Sermon Starters for 52 Sundays

CHARLES KOLLER

BAKER BOOK HOUSE

Grand Rapids, Michigan 49506

Sermon outlines numbered 25-48
were taken from *Sermon Starters,*
copyright 1973 by
Baker Book House

Copyright 1982 by
Baker Book House Company

ISBN: 0-8010-5440-0

Printed in the United States of America

Contents

SPECIAL DAYS OF THE YEAR

YOUNG PEOPLE WHO WERE A BLESSING TO OTHERS

Introduction

The lifestyle of the early church set an inspiring example of spiritual attractiveness and effectiveness — one that the modern church could well emulate. Twenty-four of the sermon starters in this book deal with early church activities: twelve are from the Book of Acts and twelve are based on the Epistle to the Philippians. These are followed by studies on the teachings of Jesus. There are also sermons for special days of the year and four sermons geared especially to youth. Today's preacher will find not only a solid core of sermon starters here, but a wide variety of topics as well.

These "sermon starters" are structured in a basic pattern* with a thesis or major thrust, an expressed or implied interrogative, and a keyword pointing directly to each main point. The thesis and key word are spelled out in the concluding lines of the introduction; and the sermon structure is indicated by capitalization, italics, numerals, and the indentation of points.

These outlines can be easily abbreviated and/or adapted for individual pulpit use by omitting words and the generous use of one's own pulpit shorthand. This book is sent forth with the prayer that it will bring a real blessing to preachers and hearers alike.

Charles W. Koller

Expository Preaching Without Notes Plus Sermons Preached Without Notes (Grand Rapids, Baker, 12th printing, 1981).

1. Ten Days in the Upper Room

Acts 1:1-14

INTRODUCTION

1. *In Old Testament times the most eventful season was from Passover to Pentecost.*

    (1) First, the Passover, celebrating Israel's deliverance from Egyptian bondage.

    (2) Then, fifty days later, Pentecost, the harvest festival, with ceremonial offering of the first fruits.

2. *In the earthly life of Jesus the most eventful time was the same period.* This time span included the Lord's Supper, crucifixion, resurrection, many appearances, the Great Commission, final instructions, and the ascension.

3. *In the life of the early church this period looms large*, with the disciples scattered, reunited, and revived.

    (1) The preparation for the miracle of Pentecost was like Elijah's preparation for the miracle of Mount Carmel (1 Kings 18:17-39). Not until the altar was built and the offering prepared and placed upon the altar, did "the fire of the Lord" fall from heaven.

    (2) The preparation for Pentecost fulfilled the unchanging *CONDITIONS* for spiritual revival.

I. A TIME OF WAITING

1. *"Go," said the Lord Jesus* in the Great Commission.

    (1) "Go ye therefore, and teach all nations" (Matt. 28:19).

    (2) "Go ye into all the world, and preach the gospel" (Mark 16:15).

    (3) "Ye shall be witnesses unto me. . . ." (Acts 1:8).

7

2. *"Wait,"* said the Lord Jesus — no less important than the command to "go."

    (1) "Wait for the promise of the Father" (v. 4).

    (2) "Tarry ye in Jerusalem, until ye be endued with power. . . ." (Luke 24:49).

3. *Waiting would not come easy for such as Peter*, with his knowledge of the life, death, resurrection, later appearances, and ascension of Jesus.

    (1) Without waiting for the Holy Spirit, Peter's sermon would have been in vain.

    (2) Without the Holy Spirit, no clever devices can revive the church.

II. A TIME OF FELLOWSHIP

1. *In one place.*

    (1) Mentioned as "the upper room" (Acts 1:13).

    (2) Remembered as a place of hallowed associations: the Lord's Supper (Mark 14:15); Resurrection Day (Luke 24:33); eight days later (John 20:26).

2. *With "one accord."*

    (1) All 120 hearts beating in unison (1:14; 2:1).

    (2) All differences reconciled — Christ's concern (Matt. 5:23-24; 18:15-17).

3. *With one devotion.*

III. A TIME OF PRAYER

"They continued with one accord in prayer and supplication" (v. 14).

1. *The distinction of "prayer and supplication"* is between worship and petition.

2. *The same distinction occurs in the Lord's Prayer* (Matt. 6:9-13).

    The first half exalts the sovereignty of God; the second half reflects the needs of man.

3. *The prayer life of the dedicated believer calls for a further element —thanksgiving* (Phil. 4:6-7).

4. *The divine intent makes prayer not a mere act, but an attitude and a way of life* that says, "Speak, Lord; for thy servant heareth" (1 Sam. 3:9).

IV. A TIME OF SHARING

1. *They had much in common when they began in the upper room.*

   (1) Their need for forgiveness, with much to confess.

   When Jesus had been betrayed, and was taken from Gethsemane, "all the disciples forsook him, and fled" (Matt. 26:56).

   (2) Their need for strengthening. "When thou hast turned back again, strengthen thy brethren" (Luke 22:32).

2. *They had much more in common "when the day of Pentecost was fully come."*

   (1) On that day they were "filled with the Holy Spirit" — conclusive evidence of repentance and forgiveness (2:4).

   (2) Afterwards, "they . . . did eat their meat with gladness. . . . And the Lord added to the church. . . ." (2:46-47).

   All the while they were setting a pattern for future generations.

   Years ago there was a sweeping revival at Northern Baptist Seminary in Chicago. It began in one of the daily chapel services with about three hundred people present. When the speaker came to the pulpit to give his message, someone stepped up and quietly informed him that two students just returned from Wheaton College were telling of a real revival taking place out there. "Shouldn't we ask them to tell us about it?" This was done. Moments later there were spontaneous prayers, interspersed with Scripture quotations, hymns and choruses, confessions and public apologies. This continued from 10:45 a.m. till 6:00 p.m. The noon meal was completely omitted. After supper the chapel was filled again and spontaneous participation continued till midnight.

Throughout, all was quiet and orderly, under the leading of the Holy Spirit. It seemed unthinkable that there could have been so many hidden differences and unsolved problems in such a dedicated seminary family. Without confession and restitution and reconciliation there can be no revival.

CONCLUSION

1. *Do we have a real longing for revival such as that of Pentecost?*
2. *Are we willing to pay the cost of Pentecost?*

2. The Church at Its Best

Acts 2:41-47

INTRODUCTION

1. *The first church at Jerusalem got off to a wonderful start.*

    (1) The leaders were with Jesus throughout His public ministry (1:21-22).

    (2) The nucleus of 120 experienced the blessing of those ten days in the upper room (1:14-15).

    (3) The enlarged membership came through the miracle of Pentecost, with vivid memories that time could not erase.

2. *The church at Jerusalem had a continuing pattern of spiritual sharing,* which accounts for its phenomenal fruitfulness.

    (1) They were living the abundant life which Jesus had promised (John 10:10).

    (2) They were experiencing the joy of the Lord in all its fullness (vv. 46-47).

    (3) They were sustained by four invincible *FACTORS* which are clearly identified.

I. THEY CONTINUED STEADFASTLY IN THE APOSTLES' DOCTRINE

1. *The apostle Peter preached, at Pentecost, the essential doctrines of the Christian faith*: the Messianic identity of Christ, His sinless life, His atoning death, His bodily resurrection, and His eternal sovereignty.

2. *The apostle John emphasized the same truths sixty years later, in the Book of Revelation* (Rev. 1:17-18).

3. *The church that continues "steadfastly in the apostles' doctrine" is the church at its best.*

    What the bones are to the body, doctrine is to the church. "Indoctrinate, or disintegrate." This is the verdict of church his-

11

tory. Dr. Charles R. Brown points this out in his memorable tract, *Who Is Jesus Christ?* "Those branches of the Protestant church which have held steadily to the higher view of Christ seem to have had the wind and tide with them." The higher view is that of the apostles. The lower view of Christ makes Him "a great man, a matchless teacher, a perfect example, a moral hero, but only a man."

II. THEY CONTINUED STEADFASTLY IN THE APOSTLES' FELLOWSHIP

1. *Here is evidence of a common devotion.*

   (1) The apostle John explains this in his Epistle: "Every one that loveth him that begat loveth him also that is begotten of him" (1 John 5:1).

   (2) The apostle Paul speaks of "the body of Christ" as members "fitly joined together," and calls for fellowship at its best (Eph. 4:16, 32).

   (3) The believers at Pentecost were "filled with the Holy Spirit" (Acts 2:4). "The fruit of the Spirit is love, joy, peace. . . ." (Gal. 5:22).

2. *Here is a need which never has changed* — the need for Christian fellowship.

   (1) This need is expressed in one of the most beloved hymns ever written: "Blest be the tie that binds our hearts in Christian love. . . ."

   (2) This tie is the only tie that really binds.

   Modern history has borne this out again and again. In a certain wartime concentration camp the captives, under severe persecution, were bound together by common suffering. But when the war was over, the concentration camp became a camp of displaced persons, it became a scene of ceaseless quarrels and conflicts. Allies who had faced a common enemy in war, became enemies to one another after victory. And individuals who are drawn together by their common dislikes have found that such friendships are more imaginary than real.

3. *Here is the world's only hope for "peace on earth."* The believers at Pentecost spoke seventeen languages (vv. 6-11), but the language of the heart was one and the same.

III. THEY CONTINUED STEADFASTLY IN THE BREAKING OF BREAD

1. *This would include the formal observance of the Lord's Supper.*

   (1) In grateful remembrance of the Savior's sacrifice. "This do in remembrance of me" (1 Cor. 11:24).

   (2) In thoughtful introspection, "Let a man examine himself. . . ." (1 Cor. 11:28).

   (3) In confident anticipation. "Till he come" (1 Cor. 11:26).

2. *This would also include visiting and spiritual sharing from house to house.*

IV. THEY CONTINUED STEADFASTLY IN PRAYER

1. *United prayer was a mighty factor in preparing the 120 for Pentecost.* "These all continued in prayer and supplication" (Acts 1:14).

2. *United prayer has the promise of added power where two or three agree* (Matt. 18:19-20).

3. *United prayer, in the spirit of the Lord's Prayer, will reconcile any two people on earth* (Matt. 6:12).

CONCLUSION

This chapter about "the church at its best" comes to a happy ending.

1. *The believers rejoiced* (v. 46).

2. *The people on the outside responded.* "Behold, how these Christians love one another!"

3. *"The Lord added to the church daily. . . ."* (v. 47).

3. They Had Been with Jesus

Acts 4:5-14, 18-21

INTRODUCTION

1. *Peter and John had just spent their first night in prison.*

2. *Peter and John did not give the usual impression of men just out of prison.*

    Noting their utter fearlessness, the authorities "took knowledge of them, that they had been with Jesus" (v. 13).

3. *Peter and John bore the family resemblance which is evidence of a family relationship with Christ.*

    How different from that night when Peter "followed afar off" (Luke 22:54)!

4. *Peter and John gave those EVIDENCES of union with Christ which should characterize every Christian.*

I. THEIR ZEAL
"They were filled with the Holy Spirit" (v. 8).

1. *They were moved with the compassion of Jesus.* "Let this mind be in you, which was also in Christ Jesus" (Phil. 2:5).

    They had seen Jesus attending the afflicted, and weeping over the city of Jerusalem (Luke 19:41).

2. *They were sustained by vivid memories of the crucifixion, resurrection, and ascension of Christ.*

    They had received the Great Commission apparently not less than three times: "preach the gospel" (Mark 16:15); "teach all nations" (Matt. 28:18-20); "be my witnesses" (Acts 1:8).

II. THEIR POWER
"By what power . . . have ye done this?" (v. 7).

1. *A Spirit-filled Christian is never powerless*, but this power is not entrusted to all.

2. *A nominal Christian gives no evidence of having been "with Jesus"* (v. 13).

Prayer can be a mere formality, and participation in the Lord's Supper might be without actual communion with Christ. Example: Once a group of deacons who had just served the elements in a communion service began to quarrel while they were clearing away the utensils.

III. THEIR BOLDNESS
"When they saw the boldness of Peter and John . . . they marveled . . ." (v. 13).

1. *Their boldness was something far better than bravery.*

   (1) Bravery is not to be despised. All honor to the brave who hold on, though with fear and trembling!

   (2) But bravery at best is only the poor refuge of those who have nothing better.

2. *Their boldness, to which we too are called, was the fearlessness of the psalmist* (Ps. 27:1).

   (1) "Fear not, little flock. . . ." Jesus said to His disciples (Luke 12:32).

   (2) There are said to be 365 "Fear nots" in the Bible, though not always expressed in these words. All are addressed to believers. These are not exhortations to be brave. Far better, they give assurance that our resources are greater than our need, and our defenses greater than any perils that threaten.

IV. THEIR PERSEVERANCE
"For we cannot but speak. . . ." (v. 20).

1. *What an inspiration to see Peter and John resuming their service to Christ.*

2. *What an inspiration to read their inspired writings of thirty to sixty years later.*

Suppose the apostles Peter, John, and Paul had weakened and given up as a result of persecution, beatings, stonings, imprisonments, and the threat of death. What a disaster that would have been to the Christian cause and to a lost world. And today, after nearly two thousand years, there would be no Epistles of Peter; and none of the fifty chapters by the apostle John, including his Epistles, the Book of Revelation, and the Gospel of John which contains the most quoted verse in the Bible (John 3:16). Nor would there be any of the precious heritage of one hundred inspired chapters from the apostle Paul.

3. *What an inspiration to see mature Christians who have weathered many storms!*

What is the secret of their endurance? There is a hidden source of strength. Some years ago I spent a week lecturing in a Bible College in Canada. The temperature was 20 degrees below zero, and a foot of snow covered the ground. During the weekend I observed, from my window, a student go out to his car with a shovel and a suitcase. I wondered how he would ever get his car started after such a frigid week and in such deep snow. The student did a good bit of shoveling; then he sprang into his car and a moment later he backed out and was on his way. Later, I learned his secret: beneath the snow was an extension cord which connected his engine to an electrical outlet, keeping the engine warm and ready to go, regardless of the length and severity of the freeze.

CONCLUSION

They "took knowledge of them that they had been with Jesus."

1. *To give this impression there must be reality in our union with Christ.*

2. *To make our witness effective our cup must be overflowing.*

4. Not Far from the Kingdom

Acts 5:26-42

INTRODUCTION

1. *The apostles created quite a stir in Jerusalem.*

   (1) They proclaimed the gospel of the crucified and resurrected Christ—a rebuke to His slayers, and a double offense to the Sadducees, who rejected the doctrine of life after death.

   (2) They were winning multitudes to Christ, and were accused of "filling Jerusalem" with their doctrine (v. 28).

2. *The council made every effort to silence the apostles.*

   They had threatened them, and were now minded "to slay them" (v. 33).

3. *The advice of Gamaliel saved the lives of the apostles.* "If this counsel be of men, it will come to naught: But if it be of God, ye can not overthrow it" (vv. 38-39).

   (1) His conclusion suggests that he might be like that other scribe to whom Jesus had said, "Thou art not far from the kingdom of God" (Mark 12:34).

   (2) His conclusion raises two *QUESTIONS* which might be helpful today to good people who are "not far from the Kingdom."

I. WHAT WAS THE STRENGTH OF HIS POSITION?

1. *He was calm in the midst of agitation and blind wrath.*

   (1) A decided advantage in every crisis.

   > "Study to be quiet" (1 Thess. 4:11).
   > ". . . be swift to hear, slow to speak, slow to wrath" (James 1:19).

   (2) A characteristic by which he had risen to leadership in that turbulent generation.

2. *He was tolerant in the presence of bigotry and fanaticism.*

Tolerance was not a common virtue in that era of persecution and violence.

3. *He was well-informed —a "doctor of law" with Roman and Jewish credentials.*

He knew the history of his people and ill-advised movements which had failed.

4. *He was prudent with the wisdom of mature years.*

He realized that ultimately the truth of God would prevail.

II. WHAT WAS THE WEAKNESS OF HIS POSITION?

1. *His calmness apparently was the calmness of the living dead* whose souls have ceased to react to the gospel, and from whom the promptings of the Holy Spirit have been withdrawn.

Perhaps there had been a time when he trembled under the impact of the gospel.

2. *His tolerance was the tolerance of indifference.*

The man farthest from the kingdom is the man standing unconcerned in the sidelines, like Gamaliel. However, sometimes apparent indifference is merely a cover-up to hide an intense inner struggle. On the opening night of a series of special services, the visiting minister was sharply criticized by one attendant. For a number of days there was no response to the messages. When the break came, the first to respond was the man who had been so bitterly critical. His intense heart-struggle was the result of concern, not indifference.

3. *His knowledge, though vast and impressive, was deficient at the most vital point.*

Gamaliel's "if" indicates that he had never bothered to investigate the validity of the gospel. And ignorance is no excuse. "If any man willeth to do his will, he shall know. . . ." (John 7:17). A noted scholar of our generation made the observation that "a man with a knowledge of the Bible and nothing else would have a far better education than a man who knows all else but not the Bible." Such was the case with the illiterate wood-cutter who was always radiant and happily in place when the church door opened.

4. *His prudence was the prudence of the "natural man"* (1 Cor. 2:14).

(1) To refrain from violence to the disciples, even a benevolent neutrality, was not enough.

(2) To do nothing is no less fatal than to *resist* the gospel (Matt. 7:21).

CONCLUSION

1. *Gamaliel apparently was "not far from the kingdom," but had a choice to make before he could enter in.*

2. *Others, "not far from the kingdom," face the same choice.*

5. A Church with a Problem

Acts 6:1-7

INTRODUCTION

1. *The trouble with the church is that it is made up of imperfect people.*

   This makes for an imperfect church and an imperfect denomination of churches.

   This does not contradict the ninety-nine biblical references to believers as "saints." Saints are still sinners, though on the way to perfection.

2. *The experience of the church in Jerusalem offers hope to every troubled church.*

   Two *ASPECTS* of this troubled situation stand out:

I. HERE WERE ALL THE ELEMENTS OF A REAL DIVISION

1. *A want of adequate organization.*

   (1) There was phenomenal growth.

   Three thousand were added on the day of Pentecost (2:41); soon there were five thousand (4:4); then there were "multitudes" added (5:14); again, the number of disciples "multiplied" (6:1).

   (2) This growth brought problems of its own.

   A man had a dream in which he saw two churches which were beset with demons. One was swarming with demons on the roof and around the door and windows. The other, across the street, had only one old demon standing guard. When the old demon was asked why one church was swarming with attention and the other almost left out, he explained: The one church was alive with activity and growth, and the other was just rocking along.

2. *An overworked leadership.*

   (1) There was the usual problem which a pastor faces. If he is

fully alert to the needs and opportunities of his field, he can only touch the high spots and ask the Lord to take care of the rest.

(2) There was the obvious want of trained assistants.

(3) There was no traditional pattern of organization from which to learn.

3. *A composite membership to assimilate* — seventeen languages spoken at Pentecost (2:5-11).

4. *An offended minority*.

Whether there had been discrimination, or only the appearance of it, the result was the same.

II. HERE WERE ALL THE ELEMENTS OF A REAL SOLUTION

1. *A dedicated leadership*.

(1) They were alert and concerned.

(2) They did not appoint helpers, but suggested that helpers be selected. The men selected were not Hebrews, but Grecians, of the offended minority.

(3) They did not reduce their own ministry of prayer and the ministry of the Word.

2. *A praying congregation* (v. 6).

3. *A willing group of unenlisted helpers*.

(1) It is often amazing to find so much unenlisted talent in the church.

(2) It was not difficult to find what this church was needing:

"Men of honest report," with merit plus reputation (1 Tim. 3:10).

"Full of the Holy Spirit and of wisdom"; the two are inseparable.

CONCLUSION

1. *Every church problem is a call to higher ground*.

Here "the word of God increased; and the number of disciples multiplied" (v. 7).

2. *Every church problem is a call for dedicated leaders and praying members and unenlisted helpers to join hands.*

Several years ago a hardworking pastor in New Jersey was distressed over the fact that his church seemed to have lost its spiritual momentum. After agonizing over the matter for many weeks, he proposed a consultation of deacons and trustees to see what could be done to revitalize the church in its internal life and its outreach. Each board member was asked to pray and to come prepared with some helpful suggestion one month hence. One suggestion, which had not been anticipated, proved to be of tremendous consequence; and that was to broadcast the Sunday evening services. This was done. The problem was solved, and the church moved into its most fruitful years.

6. The Marks of a Good Witness

Acts 6:8-15; 7:54-60

INTRODUCTION

1. *Stephen is first introduced as a man with all the qualifications of a deacon.*

   (1) He had a good reputation, with the actuality plus recognition of his worthiness. "Let these first be proved" (1 Tim. 3:10).

   (2) He was "full of the Holy Spirit and wisdom" for dealing with delicate situations.

2. *Stephen proved to be a good witness.*

   As the story unfolds, he reveals the *MARKS* of a good witness:

I. HE KNEW THE TRUTH

1. *He knew the Lord; otherwise he could not have been "full of the Holy Spirit."*

   "As many as are led by the Spirit of God, they are the sons of God" (Rom. 8:14).

2. *He knew the Word of God.* His sermon before the Sanhedrin reflects an extraordinary familiarity with Scripture.

3. *He knew the spiritual history of his people.* Their indifference to the goodness of God, their defiance of their leaders, their rejection of His Son (7:52).

II. HE LIVED THE LIFE

"Be ye doers of the Word, and not hearers only" (James 1:22).

1. *Before his ordination, he was a man "of good report."*

   The record that we write along the way remains written. Years ago I held meetings in Peoria, Illinois. At the close of one of the services, I was approached by an elderly lady who spoke as if she knew me and called me by my first name. I had no recollection of having ever seen her before. I was utterly baffled. But a moment later she introduced herself, and commented that we had not seen each other for forty-six years. I was stunned to discover that she had been a member of the little home church in Texas where I grew up, and was indeed a close eyewitness to the years of my adolescence. And now, forty-six years later, a thousand miles away, the witness turned up. How sobering to realize that our past lives on and on.

2. *Under bitter persecution, before the Sanhedrin, his face shone like "the face of an angel"* (6:15).

There was no bitter response, no fear and trembling, no desperation or despair.

3. *In his dying moments, his prayers recall the prayers of Jesus.*

(1) Jesus, on Calvary's cross, prayed, "Father, forgive them. . . ." (Luke 23:34); and finally, "Father, into thy hands I commend my spirit" (Luke 23:46).

(2) Stephen, presumably on Calvary — "out of the city" (7:58), the traditional place of stoning, "the place of a skull" (Mark 15:22) — prayed the same prayers: "Lord, lay not this sin to their charge"; and "receive my spirit" (7:59, 60).

III. HE SHARED THE FAITH

"All scripture is . . . profitable for doctrine, for reproof, for correction, for instruction in righteousness" (2 Tim. 3:16).

1. *What is profitable should be shared.* "Freely ye have received, freely give" (Matt. 10:8).

(1) The testimony of Stephen had the approval of God; therefore there was "power" and there were "miracles" (6:8).

(2) The lifestyle of the early church included much spiritual sharing — experience meetings with emphasis on prayer.

On the evening of the day of Christ's resurrection, the disciples were gathered together (Luke 24:33); then for ten days in the "upper room" (Acts 1:13); again, upon the release of the apostles from prison (Acts 4:23; 12:12).

In a challenge thirty-one years later, the same emphasis appears: "not forsaking the assembling of ourselves together ... but exhorting one another. ..." (Heb. 10:25).

2. *What is thus shared is not fruitless.*

    (1) The promise of God still stands: "... my word ... shall not return unto me void, but it shall accomplish that which I please. ..." (Isa. 55:11).

    (2) The testimony of Stephen apparently made an impact that had much to do with the salvation of Paul, the greatest preacher of all time.

    It is pleasant to contemplate that first contact, in glory, between the martyred Stephen and that "young man," Saul of Tarsus (7:58), who was "consenting unto his death, and kept the raiment of them that slew him" (Acts 22:20). There will be many pleasant surprises in heaven for parents and pastors and teachers whose labors appeared to be fruitless. "Therefore ... be ... always abounding in the work of the Lord ... your labor is not in vain. ... (1 Cor. 15:58).

CONCLUSION

1. *Stephen went to his reward with a glimpse of the glory of heaven* (7:55).

2. *Stephen left a message for all generations:* know the truth, live the life, share the faith.

7. Prayers and Prison Doors

Acts 12:1-17

INTRODUCTION

1. *This incident reflects the prevailing pattern of spiritual sharing in the early church.*

   (1) The time was about ten years after Pentecost.

   (2) The place was Jerusalem — a "cottage prayer meeting" — in the home of Mary, the mother of Mark and sister of Barnabas.

2. *This prayer meeting was in the pattern of that previous prayer meeting,* the first recorded prayer meeting after Pentecost, which moved heaven and earth (4:23-31).

   (1) In that earlier experience, Peter and John, just released from their imprisonment for preaching the gospel, had returned "to their own company."

   (2) In this later experience, Peter, upon his release hastened to the home "where many were gathered together praying" (v. 12).

   The narrative carries two helpful *SUGGESTIONS* for the prayer life of a church:

I. PRAY WITHOUT CEASING
"Prayer was made without ceasing" (v. 5).

1. *When the skies are clear and many forget God.*

   ". . . when thou shalt be full; Then beware lest thou forget the Lord" (Deut. 6:11-12).

2. *When the outlook seems hopeless* — "Be anxious in nothing" (Phil. 4:6).

   (1) King Herod, grandson of Herod the Great who had the infants of Bethlehem murdered, followed a similar pattern. He killed James and now planned to kill Peter.

(2) Peter was in prison, with elaborate safeguards to prevent his escape (v. 4).

3. *When nothing but a miracle will suffice.*

One of the greatest prayer meetings ever held, so far as I am concerned, took place when I was critically ill with diptheria at the age of five. The faithful family doctor made an added visit one evening. After a careful examination he made the sorrowful pronouncement, "The child can't possibly live through the night." Years later, my father told me the full story. When the doctor left, my father hastened across town to the home of the pastor and told him the story. With the pastor was his wife and her mother and an elderly woman visitor. The pastor replied, with confidence, "Maybe the doctor doesn't have the last word on the subject. Let's talk to the Lord about this." The five went to their knees and prayed for a miracle. Their prayer was answered. More than seventy years of excellent health have followed. The supreme fact of this universe is still, as always, "The Lord God omnipotent reigneth" (Rev. 19:6)!

4. *When God gives a negative answer.*

(1) Christ, agonizing in Gethsemane, prayed, "not my will, but thine, be done" (Luke 22:42).

(2) Paul had a "thorn in the flesh," but not without compensation (2 Cor. 12:7-9).

5. *While life lasts "men ought always to pray"* (Luke 18:1).

(1) The Christian life begins when the sinner prays, like Saul of Tarsus, "Lord, what wilt thou have me to do?" (Acts 9:6).

(2) The Christian life, in the spirit of the Lord's Prayer, calls for daily communion with the heavenly Father (Matt. 6:11).

II. PRAY WITH EXPECTATION
"They were astonished" (v. 16).

1. *God sometimes exceeds our expectations* — He is abundantly "able" (Eph. 3:20).

That prayer group apparently forgot how Peter had been delivered from two previous imprisonments (Acts 4:3; 5:18-19).

2. God makes "all things work together for good to them that love God" (Rom. 8:28).

    This assurance is followed by a complete blueprint of the believer's destiny—the foreknowledge of God, then predestination, calling, justification, glorification.

3. God mercifully discriminates between the believer's needs and his desires (Phil. 4:19).

4. God is gracious beyond all comprehension.

    "Where sin abounded, grace did much more abound" (Rom. 5:20).

    An ailing resident in a home for the aged was asked how he was getting along. "I have an inoperable cancer," he said, "and am never without pain, in spite of heavy sedation; and I have been bedridden in this condition for about two years. But these two years have been by far the happiest years of my life." Excitedly, the inquirer asked how this could be. "I attended Sunday school until I was about nine years old," he said, "then, through a combination of circumstances I dropped out completely and for the next eighty years I lived the life of a pagan. When I reached my present critical condition, in one of those endless, sleepless nights of tossing and suffering, I remembered some verses of Scripture which I learned as a child. These Scriptures became alive and meaningful, and here alone in the night I found the Lord! Now I have peace in my heart; heaven is my home; and I am waiting for my call."

CONCLUSION

1. The lifestyle of the early church has much to commend it.

2. The biggest bequest to later generations is probably its pattern of experience meetings where members shared experiences and prayer requests, and then united in prayer.

8. Each in His Own Place

Acts 13:1-5

INTRODUCTION

1. *The disciples "were called Christians first in Antioch"* (Acts 11:26).

   Three hundred miles north of Jerusalem, Antioch was the third largest city in the Roman Empire.

2. *The Christians in Antioch were the first to send missionaries to foreign lands.*

3. *The first missionaries, Barnabas and Saul, faced the question that all must answer*: What shall I do with my life?

   (1) They were "in the church" (v. 1) within calling distance, willing to be led.

   (2) Their call gives two *INDICATIONS* of the way God works in the lives of praying believers:

I. GOD CALLS EACH WORKER BY NAME
"Separate me Barnabas and Saul. . . ." (v. 2).

1. *Each is born individually, born again individually, called individually*; each performs his labors individually, dies individually, is rewarded individually.

2. *Each is unique.*

   (1) "Man is fearfully and wonderfully made" (Ps. 139:14-16); behind every atom of his being is the careful design of the Creator.

   (2) "Has your mother any more like you?" No! Neither has your heavenly Father.

3. *Each is fitted to a particular place.*

   (1) For that place, the chosen individual is the best qualified person on earth.

29

(2) A person is happiest when he is in the place God has chosen for him.

When Jonah was called of God to preach to the city of Nineveh, he was unwilling to go. He tried to flee from God, but was overtaken by the disciplinary providence of God and suffered disastrous hardship. But when he repented, God graciously reinstated him in his intended ministry; and he went on to Nineveh. There his labors were phenomenally fruitful.

II. GOD ASSIGNS EACH WORKER
TO A PARTICULAR TASK

". . . the work whereunto I have called them" (v. 2).

1. *There is only one task in which we can be completely acceptable to our Lord.*

   (1) It is no less pleasing to our Lord to be a dedicated fisherman than to be an apostle, if that is His plan.

   (2) But a called apostle is no longer acceptable or successful as a fisherman (John 21:1-6).

2. *There is only one task that will bring a full measure of blessing to ourselves.*

   A visiting preacher was invited to dinner, after the Sunday morning service, by a prosperous farmer who lived some miles out in the country. As they drove along the side of the farm, the preacher was impressed with the broad expanse of fertile fields; and as they drove up the private lane he was even more impressed with the herd of registered cattle along the way, and the beautiful house in which the family lived. When he enthusiastically expressed his admiration, he was astonished to hear the reply, "All this prosperity has left me with an empty feeling. If I were in the calling where I belong, it would be the ministry. At times, driving up this lane, it seems that even the cattle are mocking me in my embarrassment." It was not too late for some adjustments, but the bulk of his life, he felt, had been outside of the will of God.

3. *There is only one Guide who can bring us to our intended destiny.*

   (1) How gently He leads (Ps. 32:8).

(2) How beautifully His plans unfold, like lilies with hearts of gold.

4. *There is only one way that we can come to know.*

(1) "If any man willeth to do his will, he shall know. . . ." (John 7:17).

But God does not speak to unwilling ears, or reveal Himself to unwilling eyes, or come with salvation and blessing into an unwilling heart.

(2) "In all thy ways acknowledge him, and he shall direct thy paths" (Prov. 3:6).

(3) "The path of the just is as the shining light, that shineth more and more unto the perfect day" (Prov. 4:18).

CONCLUSION
In the economy of God:

1. *There is no provision for believers standing in the sidelines,* but for personal witnessing sustained by consistent living.

2. *There are no spare parts in the human body or in the church, the body of Christ.*

3. *There is a place for every believer who is willing to accept "the perfect will of God"* (Rom. 12:1-2).

9. A Controversy with a Happy Outcome

Acts 15:1-12, 22-29

INTRODUCTION

1. *The church in Jerusalem, though never equaled in spiritual attractiveness and effectiveness, was not without problems:*

   (1) Imprisonment of its ministers, Peter and John (Acts 4).

   (2) Stoning of Stephen (Acts 7).

   (3) Persecution by the Pharisees, including Saul of Tarsus (Acts 9).

   (4) Martyrdom of James (Acts 12).

   (5) Controversy with Judaizers, which began in Jerusalem and spread to Antioch, threatened the missionary outreach.

2. *The handling of this problem reveals three FACTORS which led to a happy outcome:*

I. THEY WERE WILLING TO FACE THE ISSUE
They "came together for to consider of this matter" (v. 6).

1. *The clash was between rigid Pharisaic legalism and Christian grace, between the letter and the spirit.*

   Jesus spoke out against the substitution of ritual for godliness, so this was nothing new (Matt. 23:23-28).

2. *The controversy involved not only church membership, but salvation itself* (v. 1).

3. *The issue was sufficiently critical to produce permanent schism.*

4. *The conflict was not unlike others which ended in tragic division.*
   Schism is not the answer; let there be cooperation without compromise.

II. THEY WERE READY TO LISTEN
They "kept silence, and gave audience" (v. 12).

1. *The group sets a pattern which could save many a church from disaster.*

   (1) ". . . study to be quiet. . . ." (1 Thess. 4:11).

(2) ". . . be swift to hear, slow to speak, slow to wrath" (James 1:19). Opportunity is often missed because we are broadcasting when we should be tuning in.

2. *Peter reminds them how they met this problem five years before* (Acts 11); how the Holy Spirit had confirmed the message; and that salvation is by grace (v. 11).

3. *Paul and Barnabas rehearsed what God wrought through them among the Gentiles.*

They had a right to be heard, for they had "hazarded their lives" for the cause of Christ (v. 26).

It is said of Dwight L. Moody that one day when he was evangelizing, he was approached by a critic who said, "Mr. Moody, I don't like your kind of evangelism." Then Moody, perhaps anticipating some helpful suggestion, asked the man, "How do *you* do it?" In reply, the man made no pretense of any kind of witnessing or sharing with others. Moody graciously concluded with the comment, "I think I like the way I do my evangelizing better than *your* way of *not* doing it."

4. *James gathers the loose ends together in a formula acceptable to all*, and repeated by them years later (21:25).

III. THEY WERE RESPONSIVE TO THE HOLY SPIRIT
"It seemed good to the Holy Spirit, and to us" (v. 28).

1. *As to moral conduct, there was no question.*

2. *As to non-moral problems:*

(1) Jesus had set the example. At Capernaum, "they that received tribute" approached Peter about the payment of a tax that neither he nor Jesus was due to pay. But Jesus, aware of the implications, counseled Peter, "lest we should offend them," to "give unto them for me and thee" (Matt. 17:27). To insure happy relationships, it may be necessary again and again to go "the second mile" (Matt. 5:41). Thus the doors may be kept open for the spread of the gospel, when otherwise they might be closed.

(2) The Jerusalem church, in the spirit of Christ, elected seven Grecian deacons and thus solved a real problem (6:5).

33

(3) Paul reflects the same spirit years later.

"All things are lawful unto me, but . . . not expedient" (1 Cor. 6:12; 10:23).

"It is good neither to eat flesh, nor to drink wine, nor any thing whereby thy brother stumbleth. . . ." (Rom. 14:21).

CONCLUSION
How are church problems to be solved?

1. "Not by might, nor by power, but by my spirit, saith the Lord" (Zech. 4:6).

2. "For as many as are led by the Spirit of God, they are the sons of God" (Rom. 8:14).

3. "The fruit of the Spirit is love, joy, peace. . . ." (Gal. 5:22-23).

10. Prayer by the Riverside

Acts 16:6-15

INTRODUCTION

1. *The persons usually present were a group of women who gathered here on Sabbaths for prayer.*

   (1) The only one identified by name was Lydia, a saleswoman from the distant city of Thyatira.

   (2) The visitors who dropped in on them were Paul and Silas and Timothy and Luke.

2. *The place was by the riverside outside the city of Philippi.*

3. *The significance of this prayer meeting is threefold*:

   (1) Here is the first recorded prayer meeting on the continent of Europe.

   (2) Here is the first recorded presentation of the gospel in Europe.

   (3) Here Lydia, the first convert, sets an excellent pattern with three *FULFILLMENTS* of the design of our Lord:

I. SHE KEPT THE SABBATH

1. *She was at the appointed place of blessing on the appointed day* — no temple, but nevertheless a hallowed spot.

   (1) Here God aims to communicate with His people. "Remember the sabbath day, to keep it holy" (Exod. 20:8).

   (2) Here the believer maintains his spiritual equilibrium.

      Sabbath observance is indispensable. While regular church attendance is no proof of godliness, if a person is not observing the Sabbath it is practically certain that he is not doing anything else that a Christian should be doing — praying, reading the Bible, giving, or witnessing. And the morals and ethics of a people are directly related to the degree of Sabbath observance.

(3) Here the unbeliever is in the likeliest of all places for salvation and spiritual help.

2. *She was not deterred by*:

(1) The primitive simplicity of the place, and the want of traditional "aids to worship."

(2) The want of distinguished leadership, or poor attendance, or the absence of men.

(3) The demands of business.

In my old hometown, for many years, there were two competing service stations on opposite corners. They had always been open seven days a week. One day, to the surprise of all, one displayed a new sign in front: "Customers, please get your service and supplies on Saturday. Hereafter, I am closing and going to church on Sunday." A familiar reaction was this: "That young fellow can't get away with this; his competitor will soon have his customers and he will be out of business." Several years later, that young man had doubled the size of his establishment, purchased the competitor's service station, and returned the property to its former residential status. "Them that honour me I will honour," saith the Lord (1 Sam. 2:30).

II. SHE FOUND THE LORD

1. *The Lord opened her heart* (v. 14).

(1) She could not do this in her own strength.

"It is *God* that worketh in you both to will and to do of his good pleasure" (Phil. 2:13).

"By *grace* are ye saved," not by merit (Eph. 2:8).

(2) She "worshiped God" and "attended unto the things which were spoken."

Her attitude was adapted to God's easy way: "I will guide thee *with mine eye*" (Ps. 32:8).

2. *The Lord has opened the hearts of many others by the hard way*.

(1) It took an earthquake to open the heart of the Philippian jailor (Acts 16:26).

36

(2) It took blindness to open the heart of Saul of Tarsus (Acts 9:6).

(3) It often takes a broken heart to bring a sinner to his Lord. An unbelieving husband, grieving at the open coffin of a godly wife, may at that moment give his heart to the Lord.

III. SHE BECAME AN INSTRUMENT OF BLESSING

1. *To the group at the riverside, her presence must have been a real encouragement.*

   There are three reasons for attending church: for Christ's sake, for the sake of others, and for the sake of oneself.

2. *To "her household," whomever that included* (v. 15).

   Now she had something to share, and a concern to share it.

3. *To those four bearers of the good news* (v. 15).

   (1) She now had that spiritual discernment of which the apostle John speaks: "We know that we have passed from death unto life, because we love the brethren" (1 John 3:14).

   (2) She apparently had a commodious home and was a person of means. She was "a seller of purple," the richest of textiles.

CONCLUSION

1. *The example of Lydia is a reminder that the most powerful sermons are sometimes not preached but lived* by believers "known and read of all men" (2 Cor. 3:2).

2. *The impact of that prayer meeting should be more than a momentary inspiration.*

   What a glorious revival would result if all believers consistently attended worship on the Lord's Day!

11. Singing in the Dark

Acts 16:16-34

INTRODUCTION

1. *A more unlikely setting for a prayer meeting could hardly be imagined.*

   (1) The brutal flogging of Paul and Silas was a poor preparation for a prayer meeting.

   (2) The "inner prison" was an unlikely place for a prayer meeting — usually filthy, unlighted, evil smelling.

   (3) The midnight hour, after such a day was hardly a time for singing.

2. *Yet it was a mighty prayer meeting because God was involved.*

   Three *INVOLVEMENTS* of God are indicated:

I. GOD WAS IN THE EVENTS LEADING UP TO THAT PRAYER MEETING

1. *He was an eyewitness to the uproar which followed the miraculous deliverance of that wretched, demon-possessed slave girl* exploited by her masters.

   Here was mob violence instead of gratitude, brutality instead of love.

2. *He was the unseen Protector, "keeping watch above his own."*

   (1) He permitted what He might have prevented.

   Paul explained to the Philippians, years later, that such experiences had been "unto the furtherance of the gospel" (Phil. 1:12).

   Paul assured the Romans, likewise, that "all things work together for good to them that love God" (Rom. 8:28).

   (2) He fixes limits beyond which even a demon-crazed mob may not go.

   "Hitherto shalt thou come, but no further" (Job 38:11).

II. GOD WAS IN THAT PRAYER MEETING

1. *Paul and Silas were the only persons visibly present*, but "where two or three are gathered together in my name, there am I in the midst of them" (Matt. 18:20).

2. *God moves into the night with one miracle after another.*

   (1) In the days of Job (1520 B.C.) it was written that God "giveth songs in the night" (Job 35:10).

   (2) In the darkest night of the earthly life of Jesus, just before Gethsemane, He sang a hymn with His disciples (Matt. 26:30).

   (3) Today believers do well to follow the counsel of Paul: "Speaking to yourselves in psalms and hymns and spiritual songs, singing and making melody in your heart to the Lord" (Eph. 5:19).

   An elderly Christian woman who had been losing sleep because of continuing discomfort, found something more satisfying than sleeping pills for dealing with her problem. She knew many hymns from lifelong church attendance and began silently "singing to herself" until she became drowsy and fell asleep. Another innovation was to quote Scriptures from memory until sleep came.

3. *Prisoners heard what they had never heard before*: fellow-prisoners at midnight singing "praises unto God" (v. 25).

III. GOD WAS IN THAT EARTHQUAKE

1. *He was opening the prison doors for Paul and Silas.*

   (1) He reveals His discriminating use of almighty power; the earthquake could have reduced the prison to rubble, burying all the inmates.

   (2) He reveals His complete control over all the persons involved; none seized the opportunity to escape.

2. *He was opening the heart of the Philippian jailor.*

   (1) The jailor emerges with fear and trembling.

39

How like the calloused centurion at the crucifixion of Jesus. "Truly this was the Son of God!" (Matt. 27:54).

How different from the man that he had been. When Paul and Silas were placed in his custody he did not conduct them to a convenient cell, but with needless cruelty he "thrust them into the inner prison, and made their feet fast in stocks" (v. 24).

(2) The jailor became a brother in Christ — kind, hospitable, believing, and rejoicing (v. 34).

CONCLUSION

1. *Can we sing when the night is dark and we have been mistreated?*

2. *Have we been missing something precious that Paul and Silas had in their hearts?*

12. Life in an Apostolic Church

Acts 20:17-21, 27-32

INTRODUCTION

1. *Paul reviews his ministry in Ephesus,* covering about three years.

   Here the Christian faith had so spread, and dealers in souvenirs of idolatry had lost so much business, that they had created a mighty uproar in the city.

2. *Paul reveals how this impact upon the city was accomplished.*

   (1) He speaks of his own part in the movement.

   (2) He leaves no doubt as to the lifestyle of that church in Ephesus, which was so much like that of the church in Jerusalem in the days of its greatest spiritual attractiveness and effectiveness (Acts 2:46-47).

3. *Paul shows, in six arresting phrases, the way to such spiritual power.*

   Here are six *REFLECTIONS* of total commitment to the task of spiritual sharing:

I. "ALL SEASONS" (v. 18)

1. *The Spirit-filled life is constant,* like an ever-flowing spring (Isa. 40:31; Ps. 1).

2. *The temperature of a Spirit-filled life is constant,* like that of a healthy body. It does not fluctuate between lukewarmness and fever.

3. *The concern of a Spirit-filled life is not occasional or seasonal but perennial.*

4. *The fruitage of a Spirit-filled life is constant.*

   The perfect symbol is that of a certain type of orange tree which has buds, blossoms, and fruit on the tree at the same time.

II. "ALL HUMILITY" (v. 19)

1. *How easily Paul could have weakened his ministry* by parading his distinguished pedigree, his broad learning, his phenomenal achievement.

41

With total dedication, he had been "made all things to all men," that he might "by all means save some" (1 Cor. 9:22).

2. *How indispensable humility is in the spread of the gospel, God and man testify.*

   (1) "God resisteth the proud, and giveth grace to the humble" (1 Peter 5:5).

   (2) Man distrusts and resents pride. "By pride cometh contention" (Prov. 13:10).

III. "ALL THE COUNSEL OF GOD" (v. 27)

1. *"All Scripture is . . . profitable* for doctrine, for reproof, for correction, for instruction. . . ." (2 Tim. 3:16).

2. *"All Scripture" suggests a balanced presentation of the truth.* Hobby riding produces cranks, controversies, schisms; an unbalanced diet produces unsymmetrical saints.

IV. "PUBLICLY AND FROM HOUSE TO HOUSE" (v. 20)

1. *Either without the other is incomplete.*

2. *Together they lead to abundant fruitage* (Acts 2:42-47).

   (1) Forsake not "the assembling of ourselves together" (Heb. 10:25).

   (2) Neglect not the visitation of those in affliction (James 1:27).

V. "JEWS AND GREEKS" (v. 21)

1. *The cosmopolitan character of Paul's churches is clearly evident.*

   (1) In his Epistle to the Romans Paul says, "There is no difference between the Jew and the Greek . . . the same Lord over all. . . ." (Rom. 10:12).

   (2) In his first Epistle to the Corinthians he says, "By one Spirit are we all baptized into one body . . . Jews or Gentiles . . . bond or free. . . ." (1 Cor . 12:13).

2. *The ideal congregation would be a cross section of society.*

   (1) Many languages, "out of every nation," filled with the Holy Spirit (Acts 2:4-11).

   (2) Every level of society, from slave to slavemaster, adjusted to one another by the indwelling Holy Spirit (see Philemon).

VI. "NIGHT AND DAY" (v. 31)

1. *Many are not reachable in the daytime.*

2. *Many of the unreached are preoccupied with merchandising or shopping on Sundays.*

   Night and day services might be the salvation of many. A new pastor in a metropolitan area was informed that there was an overwhelming sentiment for discontinuing the Sunday evening service. "There are sixteen churches along the miles of this street, and ours is the only one that has held on to the evening service; the other fifteen churches can't all be wrong." The pastor replied that the fifteen churches with the lights out might be fifteen reasons for their church to remain open. It was decided to try a while longer. With added emphasis and effort, the Sunday evening service became the principal means of growth, and this church outgrew all the others in the years that followed.

CONCLUSION

1. *Such is life in a truly apostolic church*; more is not possible, less is not adequate.

2. *Such is the need for today*: not new sources of power, but reopening of old wells.

13. I Have You in My Heart

Philippians 1:1-11

INTRODUCTION

1. *Prayer is the decisive test of the heart.*

   Before others one might pretend; before God one reveals his true self.

2. *Prayers of intercession are the highest possible expression of love.*

   (1) Out of a loving heart, how natural to invoke the blessing of God upon those whom we love.

   (2) "Out of the abundance of the heart the mouth speaketh" (Matt. 12:34), and the prayers ascend.

3. *The prayers of the apostle Paul reflected a profound affection* for the believers in Philippi.

   (1) He says, "I have you in my heart . . . I long for you . . . I pray for you . . . I thank God upon every remembrance of you."

   (2) He emphasizes two essential *ELEMENTS* of a healthy prayer life:

I. THE ELEMENT OF THANKSGIVING (vv. 3-8)

1. *Thanksgiving for their fellowship in the gospel* (v. 5).

   (1) That happy beginning ten years before (Acts 16:12-34).

   (2) Those later contacts, visits, gifts (4:16-18).

   (3) An unfailing resource in lonely hours, which must have been many (v. 3).

   A prominent Christian leader traveling in the Orient spent several days in one of the world's most densely populated areas where Christians were almost nonexistent. Mingling with the multitude, he felt such loneliness as he had never experienced. He came home with an appreciation of

Christian fellowship that he had never known before. "Blest be the tie that binds our hearts in Christian love."

2. *Thanksgiving for the continuing work of grace in their hearts* (v. 6).

   (1) They were "saints" (v. 1), but not without frailties and shortcomings.

   (2) They were "saints" by the grace of God (Eph. 2:8) who "worketh in you" (Phil. 1:6; 2:13).

   (3) They were "saints" on the way to perfection (v. 6).

   What God begins, He finishes (Rom. 8:29-30).

II. THE ELEMENT OF INTERCESSION (vv. 9-11)

1. *That they may grow in love, in knowledge, and in spiritual discernment* (v. 9).

   (1) Christian growth depends on Christian knowledge and understanding.

   (2) Christian knowledge depends on the willingness of the individual to respond. "He that willeth to do his will, he shall know. . . ." (John 7:17); and man is responsible not only for that which he knows, but for that also which he ought to know.

2. *That they may live up to the light that they have*, and "approve things that are excellent" (v. 10).

   Such commitment is the difference between the believer and the unbeliever.

3. *That their lives may be fruitful* (v. 11).

   (1) What are you doing for the Lord? This was a favorite question used by a counselor of seminary students to monitor their activities.

   (2) What *are we* doing for the Lord? Intercessory prayer is an area of vast potential.

   A young student pastor, serving a small church on weekends, reached a point of utter discouragement. He had never mentioned his troubles to anyone in the church. On a late Saturday afternoon he called on one of the couples of his church. As he approached the open door, he saw that the couple had sat down for an early supper and were returning thanks. A moment later he heard his name mentioned; then an earnest prayer for their "young pastor" who was "evidently burdened with some great problem." They had no inkling that he was within hearing distance; but their prayer of intercession was, to him, like a reviving blood transfusion which lifted his drooping spirit.

CONCLUSION

1. *Thanksgiving honors God and adds to the enjoyment of blessings received.*

2. *Intercession warms and sweetens all human relationships.*

14. The Fruits of Affliction

Philippians 1:12-20

INTRODUCTION

1. *Affliction did not mar the happiness of the apostle Paul.*

    (1) He was a prisoner, in chains, with an uncertain future, for the "crime" of preaching the gospel (Acts 28:20).

    (2) He radiates joy, confidence, and gratitude.

    In this Epistle there are sixteen references to "joy, rejoicing, gladness."

    (3) He gives, as his true address: "in heavenly places in Christ" (Eph. 1:3).

2. *Affliction did not mar the usefulness of the apostle.*

    (1) He demonstrates that affliction, rightly borne, makes for "the furtherance of the gospel" (v. 12).

    (2) He reveals the blessed *FRUITS OF AFFLICTION* when it is rightly borne.

I. THE GOSPEL GAINS A WIDER HEARING (v. 13)

1. *Paul's imprisonment opened a new world of contacts for witnessing.*

    (1) "In the palace" — the "saints . . . of Caesar's household" (4:22) would never have heard the gospel without this imprisonment.

    (2) "In all other places" — "Paul was suffered to dwell by himself with a soldier that kept him" (Acts 28:16). What an opportunity for unhurried witnessing.

    (3) Today and in generations past the Prison Epistles (Ephesians, Philippians, Colossians, Philemon) have been a precious part of the Bible.

2. *Paul's example is a challenge to all believers.*

    (1) Every believer a living lamp — "Ye are the light of the world. . . . let your light so shine" (Matt. 5:14, 16).

(2) Every believer a living epistle — "Ye are our epistle . . . read of all men" (2 Cor. 3:2).

(3) Every believer a living telescope, by which the faraway Savior is brought near and made visible to those who do not know Him.

II. THE BRETHREN ARE STRENGTHENED (v. 14)

1. *Strengthening of the brethren is more needed than is generally realized.*

Among the last words of Jesus to Peter, before the crucifixion: "Strengthen thy brethren" (Luke 22:32).

2. *Steadfastness under affliction is more powerful than the testimony of words.*

A name prominent in American history is that of the Confederate General Stonewall Jackson, conspicuous for his military ability and his personal virtues. He blended the devoutness of the Puritan with the severity of the soldier. He never went into a battle without prayer, and after victory he publicly gave thanks to God. In one of the great battles of the Civil War, as reported in the *International Encyclopaedia*, the South Carolinians were sorely pressed. Their commander, General Bee, to encourage his forces is said to have cried out, "Look at Jackson — there he stands like a stone wall." Thereafter, he was known as Stonewall Jackson.

(1) Paul was obviously wearing the whole armor of God — "helmet of salvation, breastplate of righteousness, shield of faith, sword of the Spirit, girdle of truth" (Eph. 6:13-17).

(2) Paul appeals to Timothy, his son in the ministry: ". . . endure hardness, as a good soldier of Jesus Christ" (2 Tim. 2:3).

(3) Paul was one of many martyrs who laid the foundations for the church of Christ, and concerning whom an early historian wrote, "The blood of martyrs is the seed of the church."

III. THE AFFLICTED IS BLESSED (v. 19)

1. *Salvation, here mentioned, covers three phases:*

(1) Redemption from the guilt and penalty of sin (Eph. 2:8).

(2) Sanctification, or growth in grace (2 Peter 3:18).

(3) Conformity to the image of Christ (Rom. 8:28-30).

Obviously, Paul was not here speaking of his new birth, or his ultimate glorification, but of the process of sanctification.

2. *Sanctification is like the polishing of precious jewels for eternity.*

On the last page of the Old Testament God speaks of the redeemed in glory as "my jewels" (Mal. 3:17).

3. *Affliction is not without compensation.*

(1) Paul's undeserved persecution brought a rewarding expansion of his ministry.

(2) Paul's "thorn in the flesh" (2 Cor. 12:7-10), coupled with the grace of God, brought strength instead of weakness.

CONCLUSION

1. *Believers can await with confidence the providences of God.*

(1) His directive providences.

"Separate me Barnabas and Saul for the work whereunto I have called them" (Acts 13:2).

(2) His disciplinary providences.

"Whom the Lord loveth he chasteneth" (Heb. 12:6).

(3) His permissive providences.

"All things work together for good to them that love God" (Rom. 8:28).

2. *Believers are counseled to make sure of their relationship to God.*

"Examine yourselves, whether ye be in the faith" (2 Cor. 13:5); if so, "be anxious in nothing. . . ." (Phil. 4:6).

15. In Christ, All Is Gain

Philippians 1:21-30

INTRODUCTION

Paul was living in the very foothills of heaven.

1. *He speaks of a real conflict in his heart:*

    (1) The desire to depart from this present life and "to be with Christ; which is far better" (v. 23).

    (2) The need to remain, with much unfinished business calling for attention.

2. *He indicates a happy escape from his dilemma* and exclaims, "For me to live is Christ, and to die is gain" (v. 21).

    (1) Prison or paradise — either alternative, if approved of God, is profitable.

    (2) Both are covered by adequate *ASSURANCES* revealed in the context.

I. TO REMAIN IS PROFITABLE

"For me to live is Christ" (v. 21).

1. *To live is to serve the cause of Christ.*

    (1) My life is an extension of the life of Christ.

    ". . . Christ liveth in me. . . ." (Gal. 2:20).

    ". . . present your bodies a living sacrifice. . . ." (Rom. 12:1).

    ". . . ye are the temple of God. . . ." (1 Cor. 3:16).

    (2) My life is a participation in the life of Christ, not just an imitation.

    "I am the vine, ye are the branches" (John 15:5).

2. *To live is to serve Christ's people.*

    (1) To the furtherance of their faith (v. 25).

(2) To the increase of their joy. What a homecoming that would be (v. 26)!

3. *To live is to prolong the privilege of witnessing and suffering for Christ.*

(1) Here he speaks of suffering for Christ as a gift (v. 29).

When Peter and his brethren were brutally beaten, they rejoiced that they were counted worthy to suffer for Christ (Acts 5:41).

(2) In another instance he declares, "Therefore I take pleasure in infirmities, in reproaches, in necessities, in persecutions, in distresses for Christ's sake. . . ." (2 Cor. 12:10).

A crippled newsboy, in the spirit of Christmas decorated his crutches with holly leaves. As he happily made his rounds on his decorated crutches he evidenced a joy that the world could not give and adverse circumstances could not take away. Such was the spirit of the apostle under persecution.

II. TO DEPART IS PROFITABLE
". . . to die is gain" (v. 21).

1. *Not death as an easy way out of a hard situation.*

(1) Paul was not one to take the line of least resistance.

(2) Paul was not taking the morbid view of one who is weary, disillusioned, discouraged, and ready to quit.

2. *Not death as an end to life, but as an incident along the way of everlasting life.*

(1) "He that believeth on the Son hath everlasting life" (John 3:36).

(2) We are assured that death does not end all; neither does it bring an uncommitted life to a happy ending.

One of the most difficult tasks of a pastor is that of holding a funeral service for an unsaved person. A woman with no church affiliation died. For many years she lived in the immediate vicinity of three active churches, none of which she ever attended. Her relatives went to the nearest pastor to arrange for "a decent Christian burial." They also arranged with a soloist to sing "Beautiful Isle of Somewhere." But there is no "beautiful isle of somewhere" for the life from which God has been left out.

3. *Not death as punishment, but as the opening of the door into God's great upper room.*

(1) The psalmist, by divine inspiration, declared, "Precious in the sight of the Lord is the death of his saints" (Ps. 116:15).

(2) The apostle Paul was given a glimpse of "heaven . . . paradise" (2 Cor. 12:2-4).

This may have occurred early in his ministry, when he was stoned at Lystra and left for dead (Acts 14:19).

Years later, he declared, "I reckon that the sufferings of this present time are not worthy to be compared with the glory which shall be revealed in us" (Rom. 8:18).

CONCLUSION

"For me to live is Christ, and to die is gain" (v. 21).

1. *The mature believer can echo this text with joyful assurance.*

2. *The mature believer can sing with confidence that beloved hymn:* "Whatever my lot, Thou hast taught me to say, it is well, it is well, with my soul."

16. Reflecting the Mind of Christ

Philippians 2:1-11

INTRODUCTION

"Let this mind be in you, which was also in Christ Jesus" (v. 5).

1. *This verse of Scripture served one remarkable preacher as text for approximately ten thousand sermons.*

   This man was black, undersized, and crippled. He began preaching at the age of eighteen and continued until he was ninety-three. He ministered to the spiritually neglected in the poorhouse, the prisons, and the chain gangs. He came to be one of the most honored and beloved persons in that city of the Old South. He said that he did not know of anything worth preaching that could not be brought under this text.

2. *This text points in two directions,* summing up the verses preceding and introducing the verses following.

   (1) There are two levels of inspiration: from Christ-like brethren, and from Christ Himself.

   (2) On the lower level, "If there be" certain graces, we are to conform; on the higher level the "if" is omitted.

3. *This text and the verses around it presents a composite pattern of Spiritual GRACES* which reflect the mind of Christ.

I. COMPASSION

"If there be therefore any . . . consolation . . . be like-minded" (vv. 1-2).

1. *Compassion goes farther than mere kindness.* "Be ye kind . . . tenderhearted. . . ." (Eph. 4:32).

   (1) To be kind is no less imperative than to be truthful, morally clean, and doctrinally sound; to be tenderhearted is no less imperative than to be kind.

Kindness is the substance of our benevolence; tenderness is the spirit and manner of communication.

(2) To be compassionate is to combine these precious elements.

Kindness may give "apples of gold"; compassion presents them in "baskets of silver" (Prov. 25:11).

2. *Compassion derives its inspiration from Christ, the head of the family,* Who was "moved with compassion" over the lost in Galilee (Matt. 9:36), wept over the city of Jerusalem (Luke 19:41-44), and prayed for His crucifiers.

3. *Compassion expresses itself in unceasing spiritual concern for others.*

II. HUMILITY
"Christ Jesus. . . . humbled himself. . . ." (vv. 5, 8).

1. *Humility rules out "striving."* "So send I you" (John 20:21). "The servant of the Lord must not strive" (2 Tim. 2:24).

   (1) When we get what we want by "striving," it has cost too much.

   (2) Two ways to do violence to the truth: deny it, or present it in such a spirit as to invite its rejection.

2. *Humility rules our "vainglory"* — excessive or ungrounded vanity (1 Cor. 4:7).

   (1) Our prerogatives are ours by grace. "By the grace of God I am what I am" (1 Cor. 15:10).

   (2) Our virtues are ours by grace. "It is God which worketh in you both to will and to do of his good pleasure" (Phil. 2:13).

3. *Humility carries with it an attitude of esteem for others.*

   (1) Everybody is superior to us in some respect.

   (2) Everybody wants to be esteemed.

   (3) Others sense how we feel about them.

   The purser on a transatlantic steamer told of an interesting experience. At the close of the first day at sea one of the passengers came to check all his valuables with the purser. "I don't know the fellow that is sharing my berth with me, but I just don't trust him," he said. Oddly enough, about fifteen minutes earlier, that "other fellow" had come to the counter to check *his* valuables, and had made virtually the same comment about *his* roommate. This mutual distrust apparently began when distrust was sensed and communicated without words.

4. *Humility seeks to understand others.* "Look . . . also on the things of others" (v. 4).

III. OBEDIENCE

Christ Jesus was "obedient unto death. . . ." (v. 8).

1. *Obedience is the essence of saving faith.*

"Not everyone . . . but he that doeth the will of my Father which is in heaven" (Matt. 7:21).

2. *Obedience is the password into the kingdom of God.*

Saul of Tarsus made the perfect response: "Lord, what wilt thou have me do do?" (Acts 9:6). This is the perfect confession of faith, the perfect rule of life, the badge of membership in the family of Christ.

3. *Obedience is the key to larger understanding.*

"If any man will do his will, he shall know. . . ." (John 7:17). God does not reveal Himself to unwilling eyes, or speak to unwilling ears, or come with salvation and blessing into an unwilling heart.

4. *Obedience is the way to Christian harmony.*

"The Lord is my shepherd. . . ." (Ps. 23). All the blessedness of this psalm rests in the responsiveness of the sheep to the shepherd.

5. *Obedience is the way to the "abundant life"* (John 10:10).

CONCLUSION

Through compassion, humility, and obedience we reflect the mind of Christ, the beauty of holiness, and the nearness of heaven to earth.

17. Going Straight in a Crooked World

Philippians 2:12-16

INTRODUCTION

"Be blameless and harmless . . . in the midst. . . ." (v. 15).

1. *Our nation inherited the enviable title of a Christian nation.*

   (1) This unique inheritance was established by the earliest colonists.

   We are reminded of the devout formulation of the Mayflower Compact, the first Thanksgiving Day, the prayerful preparation of the Constitution, the prayers of George Washington.

   (2) This inheritance was enriched by the "Great Awakening" in the eighteenth century, and the second "Great Awakening" in the nineteenth century; but there has been no "Great Awakening" in the twentith century, only outcroppings here and there.

2. *Our generation has largely forfeited its distinction as a Christian nation.*

   (1) We have had more wealth, knowledge, power, leisure, and luxury than any other people.

   (2) We have drifted to spiritual neglect, self-indulgence, and permissiveness, and have become one of the most criminal nations on earth. With crookedness, vice, drunkenness, drug addiction, and broken homes at an all-time high, our Sabbath observance, stewardship, integrity, and morality have reached an all-time low.

3. *Our generation is in the process of making a choice which can be its salvation or undoing.*

   (1) The text points the way.

   In the lobby of a beautiful motel near Shreveport, Louisiana, there was a table covered with road maps for the convenience of its guests. On the wall above the table was a small sign: "For the highway to heaven, turn right and go straight."

(2) The text implies three *OPTIONS* between which we may choose:

I. CONFORMITY TO THE LIFESTYLE OF "A CROOKED AND PERVERSE GENERATION"

1. *The chief goals in America today, according to a recent French observer,* are "success, prestige, money, power, and security."

   A French appraiser concluded that "America is great because America is good; if she should cease to be good, she would cease to be great."

2. *The prevailing philosophy seems to be, "Everybody is doing it,* and to get along you have to go along."

3. *The contrasting challenge of the Word of God is an emphatic "No!"*

   (1) "Be *not* conformed to this world. . . ." (Rom. 12:2).

   (2) "Touch *not* the unclean thing. . . ." (2 Cor. 6:17).

   (3) "Be *not* unequally yoked together with unbelievers. . . ." (2 Cor. 6:14).

   (4) "Abstain from all *appearance* of evil" (1 Thess. 5:22).

II. ISOLATION FROM "A CROOKED AND PERVERSE GENERATION"

1. *The first impulse of many true believers is toward isolation,* to avoid contamination.

   (1) Perhaps this is due to self-righteousness which says, "I am holier than thou."

   (2) Perhaps this is due to timidity.

   (3) Perhaps there is withdrawal because of uncertainty or want of conviction.

2. *The divine pattern calls for wholesome involvement and outgoing concern.*

(1) Jesus mingled with the multitude, ate with sinners, always in contact with need.

(2) Jesus commanded, "Go ye into all the world" (Mark 16:15), not just to those who are kind and lovable.

(3) Jesus prayed not that they be taken "out of the world" (John 17:15), but that they be sanctified, united, perfected.

III. SANCTIFICATION IN THE MIDST OF "A CROOKED AND PERVERSE GENERATION"

1. *The call to commitment rings out again and again.*

   "Choose you this day whom ye will serve" (Josh. 24:15).

2. *The spiritual helps for "going straight" have been provided.*

   A road map (Ps. 119:105), rules of the road (Ps. 37), a personal guide (John 16:13).

3. *The most convincing proof of total commitment is consistent Christian living.*

   (1) In the home.

   An aged minister told of the greatest thrill in his pastoral experience of more than half a century. One day he met a notoriously wicked and profane saloonkeeper on the street. Abruptly the saloonkeeper said, "Preacher, I want to be a Christian, and I want you to help me." The pastor was stunned speechless. Then came the explanation: "My wife has something that I don't have, and I want it." She had been a Christian for some time, and was consistently living the Christian life. The pastor directed this man to a completely life-changing Christian experience.

   (2) In social behavior. There is no higher compliment than to be omitted from invitations to that which is dubious.

   (3) In business. There is no conflict between clean business and a valid Christian faith.

   (4) In Christian fellowship. "We know that we have passed from death unto life, because we love the brethren. . . ." (1 John 3:14).

58

CONCLUSION

1. *Are we grieved because there is not more integrity in business*, more principle in politics, more purity in personal living?

2. *Are we "blameless and harmless . . . without rebuke, in the midst. . . ."* (v. 15)?

18. Work Out Your Own Salvation

Philippians 2:12-18

INTRODUCTION

"Work out your own salvation with fear and trembling" (v. 12).

1. *We cannot achieve our own salvation.*

    "By grace are ye saved through faith . . . it is the gift of God" (Eph. 2:8).

2. *We cannot work out a salvation that we do not possess* — no fruits without roots.

3. *We could neglect to "work out" our own salvation.*

4. *We are challenged to possess our inheritance, exercise our prerogatives, develop our potential.*

    (1) The text calls for total commitment, involving every fiber of our being — our behavior, speech, and meditation (Ps. 19:14).

    (2) The context indicates four *INCENTIVES* to such commitment:

I. IT IS PLEASING TO GOD

"It is God which worketh in you. . . ." (v. 13).

1. *God is the giver of salvation.*

2. *God supplies the impulse and enablement for every further step in sanctification.*

    (1) The voice of conscience is the voice of God — instructing, encouraging, approving; or correcting, warning, rebuking.

    (2) The believer, thus led, is like the tree "that bringeth forth his fruit in his season" (Ps. 1:3).

3. *God is pleased when His "trees" bear fruit.*

    (1) "Herein is my Father glorified, that ye bear much fruit. . . ." (John 15:8).

    (2) To please God is the supreme incentive for "working out" our salvation.

II. IT IS HONORING TO OUR TEACHERS
"... that I may rejoice. ..." (v. 16).

1. *The apostle Paul remembers, with joyful thanksgiving, the "love and faith" of Philemon* "toward the Lord Jesus" (Philem. 4-7).

2. *The apostle John expresses the same thought*: "I have no greater joy than to hear that my children walk in the truth" (3 John 4).

   (1) There is no greater compliment to a parent or teacher than to follow his or her Lord.

   (2) In comparison, the most elaborate celebration of Father's Day or Mother's Day is but a feeble gesture; and the greatest profusion of gifts is a poor substitute.

III. IT IS HELPFUL TO A LOST WORLD
"... among whom ye shine as lights in the world" (v. 15).

1. *The divine intent is for the believer to "work out" his salvation in the open*, not in secret, but "that they may see your good works, and glorify your Father which is in heaven" (Matt. 5:16).

2. *The most convincing testimony is communicated with the eloquence of godly living*.

   This was beautifully demonstrated by the patriarch Jacob, who, as a young man, lived in the household of Laban, his father-in-law, for fourteen years. When he was about to return to his own homeland, Laban tried to detain him — "I have learned by experience that the Lord hath blessed me for thy sake" (Gen. 30:27). That speaks volumes for the lifestyle of Jacob during those years.

IV. IT IS REWARDING TO THE BELIEVER
"... rejoice with me" (v. 18).

1. *We cannot honor God without being blessed in return*.

   "... Them that honour me I will honour," saith the Lord (I Sam. 2:30).

2. *We discovered, with the precious gift of salvation*, that:

   "Heaven above is brighter blue, earth around is richer green, something lives in every hue, that Christ-less eyes have never seen."

3. *We are assured that as we "work out" our salvation we are not working alone.*

"I will never leave thee, nor forsake thee" (Heb. 13:5).

CONCLUSION

1. *Paul reminds us that salvation is only the beginning,* and to "work out" our salvation is our lifelong calling.

2. *Peter, in his last recorded words, likewise appeals to believers not to stop with salvation,* but to "grow in grace" (2 Peter 3:18).

19. New Life in Christ

Philippians 3:1-12

INTRODUCTION

1. *In the economy of God many human calculations are overruled.*

   (1) The "meek" shall inherit the earth, not the aggressors (Matt. 5:5).

   (2) The band of Gideon was more formidable than the host of Midian (Judg. 7:7).

   (3) The tither receives abundant blessings, not the non-tither (Mal. 3:10).

2. *In dealing with God, we receive as we give — and vastly more.*

   (1) A star witness is the apostle Paul; few gave themselves so completely, and gained so much in return.

   (2) A comparison of two *PHASES* of his eventful life tells the story.

I. THE LIFE OUT OF WHICH HE CAME

1. *He had a distinguished background* — a "Hebrew of the Hebrews" — of the "tribe of Benjamin," like King David. He was also a Roman citizen (Acts 22:25-29), and a man of much learning (Acts 26:24).

   (1) They were a proud race, God's chosen people, with a venerable history of two thousand years.

   (2) But instead of sharing their faith they looked with disdain on non-Jews as lesser breeds, and had no dealings with the Samaritan half-Jews (John 4:9).

2. *He had an eminent position as a Pharisee*, representing the ultimate in religious attainment.

   They were literalists, who multiplied minute precepts and distinctions to the point where form was emphasized and substance was neglected. Jesus reversed this emphasis, and rebuked the scribes and Pharisees for omitting "the weightier matters of the law, judgement, mercy, and faith. . . ." (Matt. 23:23). His reference to the Pharisee and the publican at prayer in the temple reflects the pride of the Pharisee, and the inclination to shun those less holy than themselves (Luke 18:9-14).

3. *He had high moral standards* — "blameless" under the law (v. 6).

The Pharisees were meticulous in the observance of traditional regulations, but were strangers to the law of love in its all-inclusive scope.

4. *He had a great zeal for maintaining the established order* — "persecuting the church" (v. 6).

The Pharisees were self-appointed guardians, but theirs was a "zeal without knowledge" (Rom. 10:2).

II. THE LIFE INTO WHICH HE CAME

1. *He gained the "knowledge of Christ"* (v. 8).

(1) Not merely Jesus of Nazareth — "though we have known Christ after the flesh" (2 Cor. 5:16-17).

(2) Not the Christ that the unregenerate see, but the Christ who is visible to the "new creature."

2. *He gained the "righteousness which is by faith"* (v. 9).

(1) The righteousness which begins with a sense of guilt.

"Men and brethren, what shall we do?" (Acts 2:37).

"Lord, what wilt thou have me to do?" (Acts 9:6).

"Sirs, what must I do to be saved?" (Acts 16:30).

(2) The righteousness which is not earned, but imputed (Rom. 4:22-24).

3. *He gained the ability to worship "in the Spirit"* (v. 3).

(1) Worship as explained by Jesus to the Samaritan woman (John 4:23).

(2) Worship with an afterglow.

A prominent minister, reared in a Christian home, loved to tell of his mother's influence and example. They were a large family and at times things became a bit tumultuous. At these times his mother would silently disappear. In a moment she was back, serene and fully equal to the situation. Years later he found out her secret; a little time alone with the Lord completely renewed her poise.

4. *He gained the experience of rejoicing "in Christ"* (v. 3).

   (1) The "fellowship of his sufferings" (v. 10).

   (2) The hope of the resurrection (v. 11).

CONCLUSION

1. *In the old life he had zeal without knowledge, food without nourishment, muscle without strength.*

2. *In the new life he had everything that really mattered* —all else was as rubbish (v. 8). If one has the light of the sun, there is no need for the moon or stars.

20. Grace for the Imperfect

Philippians 3:13-14

INTRODUCTION

1. *This ringing challenge reveals the heart of one of the most accomplished saints in Scripture.*

   (1) On the one hand it acknowledges a deep sense of imperfection, one of the surest marks of mature Christian sainthood.

   A man of lesser spiritual discernment and attainment might have compared himself with others and concluded, "I am doing excellently."

   (2) On the other hand it expresses the hopefulness which comes with oft repeated and long continued experiences of the grace of God.

   " 'Tis grace that brought me safe thus far, and grace will lead me home."

2. *This familiar challenge comes to us with perennial freshness.*

   (1) It can vitalize the spirit for every worthy undertaking.

   (2) It gives assurance of three *KINDS OF GRACE* available to hearts rightly attuned:

I. THE GRACE TO FORGET
"Forgetting those things which are behind. . . ." (v. 13).

1. *Paul was determined to forget that which might retard spiritual service and growth.*

   (1) He mentions the sacrifices he has made—his distinguished career, his prestige and power—only to emphasize what he had gained in Christ (v. 8).

   (2) He refers to sufferings he had endured, only to point out that they were "unto the furtherance of the gospel" (Phil. 1:12).

   (3) He admits his shortcomings as one of the things to be forgotten.

2. *Paul was not denying the worth of a discriminating and retentive memory.*

    (1) He never forgot his experience of salvation and calling to the ministry. Twenty-eight years later, he told King Agrippa all about it (Acts 26:13-16).

    (2) He would emphasize that grace to remember that which strengthens is not less important than grace to forget that which weakens.

    (3) He echoes the challenge of the psalmist:

    "Bless the Lord, O my soul, and forget not all his benefits" (Ps. 103:2).

    "Pay thy vows unto the most High. . . ." (Ps. 50:14). Eight times this challenge appears in the Psalms. Vows are to be paid, not forgotten.

II. THE GRACE TO CONCENTRATE
" . . . this one thing I do. . . ." (v. 13).

1. *"This one thing" demands that the Christian "seek first the kingdom of God* (Matt. 6:33).

    This is decisive in the choice of a job, a life companion, a place to live.

2. *"This one thing" demands that the Christian "lay aside every weight"* (Heb. 12:1).

    "Harmless" involvements which have the "appearance of evil" (1 Thess. 5:22).

    "Harmless" practices which make the Christian indistinguishable from others.

    "Harmless" habits which silence the Christian testimony.

    "Harmless" activities which displace Christian worship and service.

3. *"This one thing" demands diligent application*, not casual concern, occasional gesture, halfhearted participation.

    "Whatsoever ye do, do it heartily as to the Lord, and not unto men" (Col. 3:23).

III. THE GRACE TO PERSEVERE
"I press toward the mark for the prize. . . ." (v. 14).

1. *Many good starters are poor finishers.*

   (1) Many of the young people entering college will not finish, but become dropouts along the way.

   (2) Traditional aptitude and placement tests leave out two highly important factors: perseverance and the grace of God.

2. *Many good starters despair and give up just short of the goal.*

   (1) Successful men have one thing in common: When they fall down they get up again.

   (2) Decisive battles are said to have one thing in common: There comes the moment in a battle when both generals think they are beaten. Victory is the reward of holding on a little longer.

   A pastor at a convention in New Jersey, during the Great Depression of the 1930s, looked sad beyond words. He was known as an unusually cheerful spirit. Pressed for an explanation, he told his story: "I just came through a deep tragedy. A member of my church, a prosperous real estate broker, lost everything. Times grew harder and harder, with no earnings, and no prospect of recovery. In a moment of utter despair, he took his life. The tragedy was compounded when, on the day of his funeral, there was found in his mailbox a letter from a client accepting a deal on which he had been working for months, with a commission equal to a full year's living costs for the family. If only he had held out for another twenty-four hours!"

CONCLUSION

1. *"I count not myself to have apprehended. . . ."* (v. 13). But there is grace for the imperfect.

   Motivated by divine discontent, Paul continued to grow (2 Tim. 4:7-8).

2. *"Be followers . . . of me"* (v. 17); receive grace in its fullness.

21. A Colony of Heaven

Philippians 3:13-17, 20-21

INTRODUCTION

1. *"We are a colony of heaven,"* says the apostle Paul in appealing for a lifestyle to correspond.

    (1) The message was first addressed to the church family at Philippi, a colony within a Roman colony.

    (2) The application to the church family in Philippi, or any modern city, is not difficult to see.

2. *As a "colony of heaven," we are on foreign soil* in an alien world far from home, distinguished by heavenly ways peculiar to the sons and daughters of God.

    If we are a true "colony of heaven," this raises several *EXPECTATIONS*:

I. HEAVENLY IN OUR THINKING
"Let us . . . be thus minded. . . ." (v. 15).

1. *A new believer manifests a miraculous change in his thinking.*

    (1) If any man be in Christ, he is a new creature. . . ." (2 Cor. 5:17).

    (2) "If . . . risen with Christ, seek those things which are above. . . ." (Col. 3:1).

2. *A mature believer manifests, like Paul, a growing sense of imperfection.*

    After twenty-five years of discipline, he still sees inconsistencies (Rom. 7:19, 24).

3. *A colony of believers manifests a unity of mind that has no earthly parallel.*

    (1) Paul appeals to the church family, "Let this mind be in you. . . ." (2:5).

    (2) Paul appeals to Euodias and Syntyche to "be of the same mind in the Lord" (4:2).

Attunement to the mind of Christ is the way to "peace on earth."

II. HEAVENLY IN OUR BEHAVIOR

". . . let us walk by the same rule. . . ." (v. 16).

1. *Let every life be a reflection of sound doctrine.*

   (1) Too many are long on theology, and short on character and ethics.

   (2) Too many are afflicted with the prevailing vice of the virtuous — sins of the disposition.

2. *Let every believer be a fruit bearer.*

   (1) The fruit of the Spirit is "love, joy, peace. . . ." (Gal. 5:22).

   (2) The fruit of an apple tree is apples. A friend in New Jersey had an apple tree that had been engrafted years before and was now in its prime. It bore five different kinds of apples. All were sweet and tasty, having drawn their life substance from the same source.

3. *Let every strain and temptation be a stepping stone to higher ground.*

   A leader of a huge industrial corporation made a peculiar confession. Through the years, when there had been some particularly important position to fill, he would follow this technique: At some point in his interview with a possible appointee, he would be difficult, unreasonable, and perhaps downright offensive. If the unsuspecting candidate reacted with wisdom and grace, he was appointed or promoted to the vacant position; otherwise, he was quietly dropped from further consideration.

III. HEAVENLY IN OUR FELLOWSHIP

" . . . be followers together. . . ." (v. 17).

1. *Many of heaven's richest blessings hinge on "togetherness."*

   (1) An unvarying pattern of power.

   "Where two or three are gathered together in my name. . . ." (Matt. 18:20), or 120 (Acts 2:1).

   (2) An indispensable means of keeping spiritually warm (Heb. 10:25).

Coals glowing in the fireplace turn cold and black when separated.

2. *Many believers have yet to learn the full blessing of Christian fellowship.*

   (1) We are "fitly joined together," but each must supply his own cement (Eph. 4:16).

   (2) We are to "shine as lights in the world," and to guard the lights of one another.

   In a family of six children it was a Christmas tradition for each child to put a light bulb on the tree when the time came. One day one of the children made the others angry so they decided to punish him by hiding his bulb. When all was in readiness for the lighting ceremony, the tree did not light up. To their dismay the offended five had to bring out the bulb of the offender, or remain in the dark. One missing bulb made all the difference between an unlighted tree and a joyful brightness.

CONCLUSION

1. *As a colony of heaven, we are under constant scrutiny.*

   The eyes of the world are on us, as are the eyes of heaven (Heb. 12:1).

2. *As a colony of heaven, we are to be heavenly* in our thinking, our behavior, and our fellowship.

22. God's Great Family Bible

Philippians 4:1-3

INTRODUCTION

1. *This passage reflects the warm appreciation of Paul* for his fellowlaborers in Philippi (v. 1).

   Similar expressions occur in the opening chapter: "I have you in my heart"; "I long for you"; "I pray for you"; "I thank my God upon every remembrance of you."

2. *This passage reflects also the value which God places on those "fellow-labourers* in the gospel."

   (1) "Those women" are first mentioned — Euodias and Syntyche.

   Ironically, they are singled out for correction.

   Apparently they had pronounced leadership instincts, perhaps they were individualists. Paul appeals for them to work together, to be "of the same mind in the Lord" (v. 2).

   (2) "Clement also" is mentioned — the only man called by name.

   An aged minister startled a group of listeners with the comment that in heaven the men will be heavily outnumbered by the women. He was immediately challenged, but he stood his ground. "Go to church and see for yourself. In every service the men are outnumbered. Look in the choir loft, the same is true. Check the roster of workers in the Sunday school, and the same is true. From the cradle roll through the junior department, boys and girls are equal in numbers; but after the age of twelve the percentage of boys begins to drop, and continues to decrease to the very end of life." How sad, but true. Membership statistics of our largest Protestant denomination, Southern Baptists, reveal a ratio of four to three, in favor of women and girls; and Northern Baptists have shown a ratio of three to two.

(3) Other "my fellowlabourers" are included in "the book of life," and share in the blessed *ASSURANCES* which this implies:

I. EACH FELLOWLABORER IS INDIVIDUALLY KNOWN TO HIS LORD

1. *Each is individually recorded in God's book of identification*, even before birth (Ps. 139:16).

   (1) Man is "fearfully and wonderfully made" (Ps. 139:14), suggesting careful design before the dawn of life.

   (2) God made only one of a kind; each is unique. To the familiar compliment, "Has your mother any more like you?" the answer is "No." Neither has your heavenly Father.

   (3) One is never lost in the crowd, forgotten, or mistaken for another (John 10:3, 14).

2. Each is individually recorded in "the Lamb's book of life" when born again (Rev. 21:27).

   The "Family Bible," with space for recording the birth of every new child, is beautifully symbolic of our Christian tradition.

II. EACH FELLOWLABORER IS INDIVIDUALLY IMPORTANT TO HIS LORD

1. *The Lord "hearkened"* in that time of spiritual neglect when a small, faithful minority were still conversing about the things of the Lord (Mal. 3:16).

   "Where two or three are gathered . . . there am I in the midst of them" (Matt. 18:20).

2. *The Lord caused a record to be made in the "book of remembrance."*

   Not every fellowlaborer will get into the headlines, but all are included in that "book of remembrance." Many of those in *Who's Who in Heaven* will be persons with unimpressive earthly credentials, but whose faithfulness God noted. Such a person was a handicapped young man whose mental development was halted by a near-fatal illness when he was about twelve years old. He found the Lord when he was in his middle-teens and became a pattern of dedication. He developed extraordinary prayer power and a deep concern for the salvation of others. Through him a number of people found salvation and were united with the church. All the while God took note.

3. *The Lord cherishes these fellowlabourers as "the jewelry of heaven"* (Mal. 3:17).

Here everybody is somebody, and the human cipher becomes a person of significance.

III. EACH FELLOWLABORER IS INDIVIDUALLY ASSURED OF HIS REWARD

1. *God has taken note, therefore their "names are in the book of life."*

Not one service is unnoticed, unremembered, unrewarded (Mark 9:41; 1 Cor. 2:9).

2. *God adds His blessing to every faithful service.*

Thirteen humble believers meeting in a home in rural Iowa organized themselves into a church. It seemed like nothing of consequence. But one-hundred years later it was a flourishing church of 1,300, with an amazing history of blessing along the way.

CONCLUSION
1 Cor. 15:58

1. *Life begins when one's name is inscribed in God's "book of life"* — God's great family Bible.

2. *Life gains an added dimension of blessing when we become fellowlaborers.*

23. The Peace of God

Philippians 4:4-9

INTRODUCTION

1. *Paul, in this Epistle, makes repeated references to "joy" and "rejoicing."*

   (1) This does not sound like something written by a man in prison, with no prospect of release.

   (2) This optimism continued to the very end of life: "The Lord . . . will preserve me unto his heavenly kingdom" (2 Tim. 4:18).

2. *Paul makes it clear that the "joy of the Lord" is inseparably related to the "peace of God."*

   (1) In another Epistle he emphasizes that "peace" is the "fruit of the Spirit" (Gal. 5:22), and is not unconditionally imparted.

   (2) Here he indicates the *ESSENTIALS* upon which the "peace of God" depends:

I. BE PRAYERFUL (v. 6)

1. *There must be a saving contact with God.*

   (1) "There is no peace, saith my God, to the wicked" (Isa. 57:21).

   (2) There is hope for all, as for Saul of Tarsus when he was "chief" of sinners (1 Tim. 1:15).

2. *There must be a continuing relationship with God.*

   (1) A two-way communication between two persons who love one another — the child of God, and the heavenly Father.

   This analogy reminds us that the wise parent does not always fulfill the child's request. He always answers; but the reply may be "yes," or "no," or "wait a while." To fulfill every request of the child would not be a kindness, and in some cases might be disastrous. Similarly, the child of God does not have all his requests fulfilled. Even the apostle Paul had a "thorn in the flesh" (2 Cor. 12:7-9) which he prayed to have removed. God showed him a better way, to even larger blessings than he had in mind.

(2) A promise that is still being fulfilled, "They that wait upon the Lord. . . ." (Isa. 40:31).

3. *There must be a balanced prayer life, as indicated in the traditional formula*, A.C.T.S., adoration, confession, thanksgiving, supplication.

(1) The inclusion of thanksgiving adds to the joy of receiving.

(2) The prevailing pattern makes prayer only "a celestial shopping list."

II. BE TRUSTFUL

1. *Believe the promises of God.*

(1) ". . . in everything. . . ." (v. 6). No situation is hopeless.

(2) "All things work together for good. . . ." (Rom. 8:28). This is no less true when the outlook is grim than when the sun is shining.

2. *Receive by faith the "peace of God."*

(1) "Being justified by faith, we have peace with God. . . ." (Rom. 5:1).

(2) "Thou wilt keep him in perfect peace, whose mind is stayed on thee: because he trusteth in thee" (Isa. 26:3).

The soul that is at peace with God is undefeatable. On a visit back to my hometown, I heard of the illness of a dedicated Christian friend whom I had known for more than fifty years. When I asked her how she was doing, she replied: "I have a condition which may be terminal. Sometimes it seems that I might recover. If so, I shall thank God, knowing that it was by His gracious providence. There are also times when it seems that the end is near. If so, I am fully prepared. And so, whichever happens, I can't lose."

III. BE WATCHFUL (v. 8)

1. *Our spiritual diet will produce character to correspond.* "As a man thinketh in his heart, so is he" (Prov. 23:7).

(1) Here is wise counsel for "spiritual weight-watchers."

(2) Here is the inevitable sequence: first the thought, then the act, then the habit, then the character.

2. *Our spiritual diet will motivate our behavior.*

Too many do not realize that by their choice of entertainment they are dulling their spiritual appetites.

3. *Our spiritual diet is itself subject to the judgment of God.*

To lust is to commit adultery (Matt. 5:28), and to be angry may be the equivalent of murder.

4. *Our spiritual diet will affect the lives and destiny of others.*

The most powerful sermons are not preached, but lived.

CONCLUSION

1. *"The joy of the Lord is your strength"* (Neh. 8:10).

2. *But "the joy of the Lord" is conditioned on "the peace of God."*

24. The Enabling Christ

Philippians 4:10-23

INTRODUCTION

1. *Paul, writing to the Philippians, rejoiced over their loving remembrance of him.*

    (1) It is always pleasant to be remembered by distant friends.

    (2) It was particularly thrilling to be visited in his Roman inprisonment by Epaphroditus from Philippi, seven hundred miles away.

2. *Paul rejoiced "in the Lord."*

    (1) It was the Lord who put it in their hearts thus to remember him (1:4-6).

    (2) It was the Lord who enabled him to face persecution, frustration, and suffering with composure.

3. *Paul shared the assurances which sustained him;* three ENABLE-MENTS are mentioned:

I. THROUGH CHRIST I CAN BE WHAT I OUGHT TO BE

1. *"I have learned . . . to be content"* (v. 11).

    (1) Contentment has to be learned from Him who taught it to the apostle.

    (2) Contentment is not dependent on outwardly favorable circumstances.

    It is like the happiness of the man in the first psalm, symbolized by the tree "planted by the rivers of water." This tree "bringeth forth his fruit in his season; his leaf also shall not wither. . . ." The imagery of the psalm suggests a drought-stricken landscape in which the grass has turned brown, the foliage is yellow and sparse, and the fruitless twigs are dying. But in the midst of this desolation one tree stands green, beautiful, and fruitful. It is subjected to the same withering drought, the same hot winds from the desert; but it is able to defy the elements because it is continuously nourished by the life-giving waters flowing at its roots.

2. *"By grace of God I am what I am"* (1 Cor. 15:10).

   (1) With the grace of God flowing into his soul, Paul was serenely looking toward the light.

   (2) With the grace of God lifting his spirit, Paul had something powerful that enabled him to rise above otherwise disabling circumstances.

   (3) With the grace of God changing the heart, the foulest becomes clean, the meanest becomes noble, as with the Philippian jailor (Acts 16:23-34).

II. THROUGH CHRIST I CAN DO WHAT I OUGHT TO DO

"I can do all things through Christ which strengtheneth me"
(v. 13).

1. *Christ gives strength to achieve what would otherwise be impossible.*

   (1) "Go ye . . . make disciples. . . . and, lo, I am with you always. . . . (Matt. 28:19-20).

   (2) "Without me ye can do nothing" (John 15:5). The outcome of our labors depends on that which the Lord adds, or withholds.

   > Unless Christ "strengthens," no amount of native ability, education, or hard work can compensate. Happy weddings do not insure happy homes. True love is not enough: it might be unsanctified, misdirected, short-lived. Without Christ, the best efforts will result only in failure. With Christ, the home becomes a little bit of heaven.

2. *Christ gives strength to endure what would otherwise be intolerable.*

   > "They that wait upon the Lord shall renew their strength" (Isa. 40:31), like a spring in the desert sustained by the inexhaustible waters of a distant mountain lake.

3. *Christ gives strength to face uncertainty, danger, or death.*

   > In the annals of New England there is an account of an awesome spectacle in the heavens when darkness fell at midday,

shooting stars flashed across the skies, and flaming meteors fell to the earth. Normal activities came to a standstill. Multitudes of frightened people believed the end of the world had come. In one home the maid burst into the room where the head of the house was calmly at work. Hysterically, she shrieked, "The world is coming to an end!" "Let it," was the calm reply, "we can get along without it." How true! This is what everyone *will have to do* sooner or later.

III. THROUGH CHRIST I CAN HAVE
WHAT I OUGHT TO HAVE
"My God shall supply all your need" (v. 19).

1. *"My Father is rich. . . ."* Gladly believing, we sing this hymn of faith.

   (1) He alone is able to supply our physical and spiritual needs.

   (2) He distinguishes between our *needs* and our *wants*.

2. *Paul himself was rich* (v. 18).

   (1) He had no house or lands, stocks or bonds, no place "to lay his head" (Matt. 8:20).

   (2) But, in true riches, he was probably one of the weathiest men on earth.

      In comparison, Nero on his throne with a vast empire at his feet, was poor indeed.

3. *All of God's children are rich.*

   (1) God never intended that believers should live meager lives, but come to the "abundant life" (John 10:10).

   (2) God invites believers to claim their inheritance (v. 19).

CONCLUSION

1. *Paul begins on a high note of rejoicing* (v. 10), *and concludes on the same level*, with his doxology, salutation, and benediction (vv. 20-23).

2. *Paul makes it clear that believers have cause for rejoicing* — "through Christ I can!"

25. The Law that Solves All Problems

Matthew 5:43-48

INTRODUCTION

1. *"There ought to be a law!"*

   (1) This is a familiar reaction to uncontrolled abuses. And so we grind out more laws, appoint more judges and police, multiply bureaucracies, and increase taxes.

   (2) There is a better way: Prevent abuses by removing the cause.

   A parable is told about a town in a deep valley, to which the main approach was by a road along the edge of a high cliff overlooking the town. From time to time vehicles would fall over the precipice. As these disasters increased in frequency, the town fathers decided that something must be done. And so they built a hospital at the foot of the cliff to care for the injured. But no one ever suggested a protective stone fence along that upper road to prevent vehicles from falling over the edge of the cliff!

2. *There is a law,* designed of God, to prevent abuses: the law of love (Gal. 5:14).

   (1) To change society, change the individual. No rearrangement of bad eggs will ever make a good omelet.

   (2) To change the individual, change the heart. At the heart of every human problem is the problem of the human heart (Prov. 4:23).

   (3) To change the heart, it must be related to the Source of love, righteousness, and goodness (2 Cor. 5:17).

3. *There are four APPLICATIONS of the law of love,* spelled out in the Word of God:

I. LOVE THE LORD—Luke 10:27

1. *God reaches down and takes the initiative in relating us to Himself.*

(1) To Adam, guilty, burning with remorse, full of fear, God calls out, "Adam, where art thou?" (Gen. 3:9).

(2) To Jacob, who had defrauded his brother, lied to his father, and fled for his life, God appeared in a dream (Gen. 28:12).

(3) To a world of lost souls, God sent His Son, "reconciling . . ." (2 Cor. 5:19).

2. *Man reaches up and grasps the life line* (Eph. 2:8).

3. *The Holy Spirit comes in;* the first "fruit of the Spirit" is love (Gal. 5:22).

4. *Believers confess: "We love Him, because He first loved us"* (1 John 4:19).

II. LOVE THE BRETHREN—John 13:35

1. *A proof of salvation* (1 John 3:14).

2. *A testimony that amazes and convinces*—"Behold, how they love one another!"

3. *A tie that truly binds.*

(1) The true child of God craves companionship with God's family.

A young pastor was concerned and puzzled over the continuing neglect of a certain professed Christian to unite with the church. A mature deacon offered this explanation: "That man has not been born again. If he were a true child of God, you couldn't keep him out. And if you tried, he would keep standing at the door, like a sheep bleating to enter the sheepfold."

(2) The "church covenant" used in thousands of churches begins with the promise, "by the aid of the Holy Spirit, to walk together in Christian love."

III. LOVE THY NEIGHBOR—Matt. 19:19

1. *Respect his rights and interests.* This would mean the end of all thievery, vandalism, and indifference to the rights and interests of others.

2. *Spare his feelings.* Observe the Golden Rule (Matt. 7:12; Eph. 4:32).

3. *Seek his spiritual well-being.*

(1) With outgoing concern—"freely ye have received, freely give" (Matt. 10:8).

(2) With sympathetic adaptation to find common ground, like the apostle Paul—"I am become all things to all men that I may by all means save some" (1 Cor. 9:22, ASV).

IV. LOVE YOUR ENEMIES—Matt. 5:44

1. *Three kinds of enmity:* hate smoldering in the heart, expressed in speech, or translated into action.

2. *Three ways to react:*

    (1) Retaliate. But " ... avenge not yourselves ... " (Rom. 12:19); " ... the wrath of man worketh not the righteousness of God" (James 1:20).

    (2) Deplore and ignore. But this is not the way of Christ. And God did not "deplore and ignore," but sent His Son to seek and to save (John 3:16-17).

    (3) Conciliate. Love builds bridges, reconciles, heals, and sweetens all relationships.

CONCLUSION

"The law that solves all problems"

begins with reconciliation and communion with God.

expresses itself in every human relationship (Luke 10:27).

26. The Most Important Element in Christian Living

Matthew 6:5-13

INTRODUCTION

1. *The most important element in Christian living is the prayer life of the believer.* But many professed believers are scarcely on speaking terms with the Heavenly Father. This is the world's most serious "generation gap." To many, prayer is only a pious incidental, an option to be exercised if and when the mood so dictates.

2. *The psalmist declared, centuries ago, "It is a good thing* to give thanks unto the Lord ... To show forth thy lovingkindness in the morning, and thy faithfulness every night" (Ps. 92:1-2). He had a pattern of daily devotions—morning and evening communion with the Heavenly Father.

3. *The Lord Jesus declared, "... men ought always to pray ... "* (Luke 18:1). The apostle Paul echoes this thought: "Pray without ceasing" (1 Thess. 5:17). What does this mean? Of course there must be no lapses in one's prayer life. But much more is suggested. Prayer is to be not merely an act, but an attitude, a way of life which says, "Lord, what wilt thou have me to do?" (Acts 9:6).

   (1) Jesus began His public ministry in prayer (Luke 3:21-22); and in prayer He concluded His public ministry (Luke 23:46).

   (2) Among the *PORTRAYALS of the prayer life of Jesus,* in the Gospels, two can be especially helpful to the believer who is striving for higher ground:

I. A MORNING SCENE IN THE LIFE OF JESUS

1. *How did Jesus begin His day?* In prayer (Mark 1:35).

2. *What did the morning prayer mean to Him?* It gave assurance of:

(1) Physical strength and mental freshness for the demands of the day.

(2) Spiritual reserves to fortify the soul and provide an overflow for others.

(3) Wholesome atmosphere in which to begin the day—no "blue Mondays," etc.

3. *What does the morning prayer mean to the Christian?*

(1) To check in with his Lord, like a faithful employee awaiting his orders for the day (Luke 9:23). How often? Daily. "Give us this day our daily bread" (Matt. 6:11). How early? Before the "daily bread" has been received.

(2) To set the tone for the new day. There is need for grace and guidance for all foreseeable tasks and testings, choices and decisions, responsibilities and opportunities. There is need also for spiritual reserves to meet the unforeseeable, and for long-range guidance.

A South Carolina potato farmer shared this experience: He had prospered on his original fifty acres; and with continuing prosperity he gradually expanded his operations to five hundred acres. Still he prospered. Then, with a bumper crop harvested and loaded on freight cars and started on its way to the New York market, there occurred a crippling railroad strike. As the strike went on and on, he became increasingly alarmed over the fate of those potatoes, presumably rotting on some side track along the way. Finally, in desperation, he cried to God for help. "Oh Lord, do something about those potatoes!" The response came to him like an audible voice, "What potatoes, son?" Then he realized that he had not taken God into account and had not prayed over those potatoes as he planted, cultivated, and harvested them, nor when he had them loaded for shipment. Why bother the Lord with them now? The lesson was obvious, and unforgettable.

II. AN EVENING SCENE IN THE LIFE OF JESUS

1. *How did Jesus close His day?* In prayer (Matt. 14:23).

2. *What did the evening prayer mean to Him?* Primarily it meant communion with the Heavenly Father. Prayer has been aptly defined as "a dialog between two persons who love each other."

3. *What does the evening prayer mean to the Christian?*

   (1) Communion with the Heavenly Father, coupled with thanksgiving. Every day is a gift of God, every breath we draw, every heartbeat.

   (2) Confession, coupled with petition for forgiveness, restoration, healing.

   (3) Checking out, like a faithful employee at the close of the working day.

   Years ago, before the day of electric clocks, we received as a gift a beautiful and expensive mantel clock. The winding stem was rather close to the trigger for adjusting to "Slow" or "Fast," and as a result the clock was nearly always a bit slow or fast—not strictly accurate. And yet, we lived by that clock for years. How was this possible? I had a pocket watch which was a perfect timepiece; and every night, just before retiring, it was routine to adjust the mantel clock to complete accuracy. Thus it was never far wrong—like the truly dedicated Christian—never perfect, but fully corrected each night by thoughtfully and conscientiously "checking out" with the Lord before venturing to close the eyes in sleep.

CONCLUSION

1. *In prayer we find salvation and draw our first breath of everlasting life.* It is in that moment when we fully respond to our Lord, like Saul of Tarsus: "Lord, what wilt thou have me to do?" (Acts 9:6).

2. *In prayer we nurture the spiritual life*—morning, evening, or in the middle of the night. "Speak, Lord, for thy servant heareth" (1 Sam. 3:9).

3. *In adopting the devotional pattern of the Lord Jesus,* many believers may add a new dimension of blessing to their lives (Isa. 40:31).

27. Living by the Day

Matthew 6:24-34

INTRODUCTION

1. *God purposed that we should live our lives on the installment plan.*

   (1) He measures them out to us in installments, or days.

   (2) He has devised barriers to keep the days apart.

   Darkness, falling between the days to establish this division.

   Fatigue, God's protective device against overdoing.

   Sleep, the chloroform of God, to relieve any distresses of yesterday.

   Veil of mystery hiding from view the burdens of tomorrow.

   (3) He bestows our blessings and assigns our tasks in daily portions.

   "Give us . . . daily bread" (Matt. 6:11)—daily communication implied.

   "As thy days, so shall thy strength be" (Deut. 33:25).

   "Sufficient unto the day is the evil [trouble] thereof" (Matt. 6:34).

2. *We live most wisely when we live as God intended—one day at a time.*

   (1) Our heaviest tasks become bearable.

   The young bride anticipates not less than fifty years of uninterrupted happiness. In most cases she will do her housekeeping without the help of a maid, and will wash the dishes without the convenience of an electric dishwasher. Perhaps, in her marriage vow, she is promising more than she realizes. Three batches of dirty dishes per day amount to more than a thousand per year—more than fifty thousand in fifty years! In the marriage ceremony, there always comes that decisive moment when the minister asks, "Do you solemnly promise . . ." Suppose, in that critical moment, there rises up before her, like a frightening ghost, the grim spectre of fifty thousand batches of dirty dishes in one pile—a pile as big as the church itself! She begins to tremble

87

and stutter; she shakes her head; she goes out from that service as single as she came in—determined to live and die in the blessings of spinsterhood! But the bride is smart enough to think of her dishes as so many little jobs quickly accomplished, without strain or hardship. After breakfast, all is done in a few minutes; after lunch, the task is even simpler; and after dinner, the husband will wipe the dishes (2 Kings 21:13); and how wonderful will be that fellowship around the dishpan! And so the bride says yes, and they "live happily ever after."

(2) Our common blessings retain a delightful freshness—one meal at a time.

(3) Our sufferings and afflictions become tolerable—one day at a time.

3. *We escape three KINDS OF DISTRESSES, in living by the day:*

I. THE DISTRESSES OF AN UNHAPPY PAST

1. *The ungodly luggage we sometimes carry with us:* old troubles, worries, resentments, grudges—rubbish dishonoring to God and hurtful to the soul. "Thank God for a waste basket!"

2. *The unholy emotions of yesterday*—anger, etc. (James 1:20; Eph. 4:25).

3. *The sins, errors, and omissions of yesterday* (Phil. 3:13-14).

II. THE DISTRESSES OF AN OVER BURDENED PRESENT

1. *"Be not anxious for tomorrow."*

(1) Tomorrow may not find us here. "I'm one day nearer home today than I've ever been before."

(2) Anxiety will not relieve tomorrow of its necessary tasks, testings, and disciplines; nor will it stave off the judgment of God upon sins unconfessed, unremoved, unforgiven.

2. *"Seek ye first the kingdom of God."*

(1) Our Shepherd provides (Ps. 23).

(2) Our *needs* are supplied (Phil. 4:19)—not our *wants.*

(3) Our supply comes daily; manna must not be hoarded (Exod. 16:14-26).

III. THE DISTRESSES OF AN IMPAIRED FUTURE

1. *Our lives are conducted on a limited but adequate capital.*

   (1) Excesses today dissipate tomorrow's capital of strength and resources.

   (2) Evasions and procrastinations overtax the resources of tomorrow.

2. *Our undoing: a new day already undermined and overloaded.*

   Attempting to carry three loads (yesterday's, today's, and tomorrow's), multitudes of people are breaking under the strain.

3. *Our hope: God's better plan—daily renewal of tasks, strength, resources.*

   It was on a late Saturday afternoon that I arrived at my place of lodging near the church where I was to hold a series of meetings. The area had become industrial, with factories not far away. The smog was heavy, the streets were grimy, and that beautiful old gray stone church building had become almost black. I walked around in that gloomy, depressing atmosphere, unconsciously absorbing its full effect. And so I retired for the night's rest. When I arose in the morning and looked out the window, I experienced one of the unforgettable thrills of a lifetime. A snow had fallen during the night; now the sun had risen; and a landscape of indescribable beauty and purity was shimmering in its golden glow. The air was clean, and there was nothing to suggest the pollution of the evening before. I remember exclaiming to myself, "Only God could do a job like that!" And He does it every day. Whatever our yesterdays, each new day can be a fresh beginning, with a clean, snow-white carpet rolled out before us, and with a loving Heavenly Father directing our steps and watching over His own.

CONCLUSION

"This is the day which the Lord hath made; we will rejoice and be glad in it" (Ps. 118:24).

1. *To His beloved child, He says, "Fear not . . ."* (Luke 12:7, 32).

2. *To others, He says, "Come . . . "—be cleansed* (Isa. 1:18); and "I will never leave thee, nor forsake thee" (Heb. 13:5).

28. Religion Without Salvation

Matthew 7:21-29

INTRODUCTION

1. *Religion and salvation are not the same thing.*

    (1) Religion is any system of beliefs about God, and the expression of these beliefs in attitude, worship, and behavior.

    (2) Salvation is deliverance from sin and its consequences, coupled with the sweet, heaven-born assurance of oneness with God.

2. *Religion and salvation do not necessarily go together.*

    (1) Nicodemus, cultured Pharisee, teacher of religion, embodiment of highest moral and ethical standards, "must be born again" (John 3:7).

    (2) Men who crucified Christ were profoundly religious, but lost.

    (3) Paul the Apostle was never more religious than in his merciless persecution of Christians, but it was zeal without knowledge (Rom. 10:2).

    (4) Benighted pagan in the jungle is more deeply religious than most of us, as he sacrificially seeks to appease the supposed wrath of some loveless deity.

3. *The Bible speaks of "pure religion and undefiled"* (James 1:27), and commends this outward expression of devotion to Christ.

4. *The Bible speaks also of religion without salvation,* deceiving the soul, to its eternal undoing (Matt. 7:21-23).

    Three sobering PRONOUNCEMENTS, with which the Lord Jesus concluded the Sermon on the Mount, carry the message:

I. TO CONFUSE RELIGION WITH SALVATION IS A COMMON MISTAKE
"Many will say to me in that day . . . " (v. 22).

1. *The nominal Christian who goes through all the motions of church activity.*

    An evangelist of wide experience tells of the most surprising conversion he ever witnessed. At the conclusion of his message in that large church where he was holding meetings, he gave the usual invitation to Christian commitment. A middle-aged woman came forward, in deeply emotional response. When he recognized her as the president of the Women's Missionary Society of the church, and as president of the Women's Missionary Union of that state, he was utterly baffled. Then she explained. She had grown up in the church; she had received baptism in her childhood; and she had been active in leadership for years. But she had never seen herself as a lost sinner, had never repented, and had never personally come to terms with Christ as the Lord of her life and Savior of her soul. She had never been "born again." She had never had more than religion without salvation.

2. *The moralist who formulates his own plan of salvation,* and stakes his destiny on the expectation of salvation without a Savior.

   (1) "I am already a Christian," says one, not realizing that a saving faith is of necessity the response of a person to a Person.

   (2) "My religion is the Golden Rule," says another. But suppose he lives a thousand years without injury or offense to others! When all have died, there remains the Eternal One to whom he has never related himself.

   (3) "I am not good enough to go to heaven, and not bad enough to go to hell." The answer is best expressed in the words of Jesus: "Depart from me." There is a place prepared for everyone (Matt. 25:41).

   (4) "I'll take my chances—I live clean—I treat everybody right." No, he is not taking chances; he is destroying the one and only chance that he has.

   (5) "If I go to hell, I'll have lots of company." Yes, there will be "many," says Jesus. But what a company with whom to spend eternity, in that wretched abode of the doomed, that cesspool of depravity, with its aggregation of filthy human degenerates from whom the Holy Spirit has forever departed, and whose movements are forever subject to the power of evil spirits!

II. TO CONFUSE RELIGION WITH SALVATION IS A DANGEROUS MISTAKE
"Not every one . . . shall enter into the kingdom" (v. 21).

91

1. *It may blind the unbeliever to his real need.*
   Cf.: The virtuous Pharisee and the guilty Publican—(Luke 18:9-14).

2. *It may lead to infidelity.*
   The renowned B. H. Carroll grew up with all the advantages of Christian training and environment. When others of his age united with the church, he went along with the crowd, but without any true experience of saving faith. Later on, as he heard others testify of their faith, he thought they were hypocrites. Rather than to live as a hypocrite, he withdrew from the church, and began to rationalize and justify his conclusions. He became a blatant infidel, brilliantly expounding his views. After the Civil War, wounded and disillusioned, he was back in his hometown, with a woeful emptiness in his heart. In his famous message, "My Infidelity and What Became of It," he tells how he came to see the light, and emerged from the disappointing twilight of religion without salvation to the "peace of God which passeth all understanding" (Phil. 4:7).

3. *It may lead to the ultimate disaster—*"Depart from me . . . " (v. 23).

III. TO CONFUSE RELIGION WITH SALVATION IS AN UNNECESSARY MISTAKE
" . . . he that doeth the will of my Father . . . " (v. 21; John 7:17).

1. *The Word of God is plain—*Why call ye me Lord, Lord, and do not . . . " (Luke 6:46).

2. *The voice of conscience confirms the written Word.*

3. *The conclusive test of a saving relationship:* a life built around the prayer, "Lord, what wilt Thou have me to do?" (Acts 9:6)

CONCLUSION

"Examine yourselves, whether ye be in the faith; prove your own selves" (2 Cor. 13:5).

29. The Rhythm of the Abundant Life

Matthew 9:35-38; 10:1, 5-8

INTRODUCTION

1. *This is the rhythm of the abundant life*—receiving, giving. "Freely ye have received, freely give" (Matt. 10:8).

   (1) It was never intended that we should

   Live spiritually meager, undernourished, stunted little lives (John 10:10).

   Remain in spiritual adolescence, growing old but never growing up (2 Peter 3:18).

   Build tiny structures on the skyscraper foundation laid for us (1 Cor. 3:11).

   (2) It was never intended that we should

   Come into the church as spectators, but as full participants.

   Hibernate between Sundays, but communicate!

   A department superintendent was enthusiastically telling his pastor, "I have just learned from one of the fellows with whom I work that he too is a department superintendent in Sunday school, and is as deeply involved there as I am here!" The pastor was delighted. Then he asked, "How long have you been working with this man?" When informed that it had been about three months, the pastor really exploded. "What's wrong with both of you! How could either of you care so little as to go this long without finding out whether the other fellow is saved and on his way to heaven, or lost and on his way to a Saviorless and hopeless eternity?"

2. *Here are the ESSENTIALS by which we are to test our lives:*

I. AN ADEQUATE SPIRITUAL INTAKE
"Freely ye have received."

1. *This calls for an open channel to the throne room of heaven.*

(1) The channel opens, and communication is established, when the soul comes to terms with God (Acts 9:6).

(2) A new creature is born (2 Cor. 5:17).

(3) The soul's deepest hunger is satisfied.

Saint Augustine expressed in his prayer what every true believer experiences: "Thou hast made us for Thyself, oh God; and our hearts are restless till they find their rest in Thee."

2. *This calls for a continuous inflow of grace and strength* (Isa. 40:31).

(1) Christian annuitants, with the benefit of this continuing inflow, are known to live appreciably longer than others.

(2) Women live longer than men. The reason is clear: Prayer life and church attendance usually go together, and seldom is the number of men in church equal to the number of women.

(3) Marriages last longer when there is commitment and communion in the spirit of this text. A famous news commentator, reporting on a vast number of couples that had been "happily-ever-aftering" for sixty years or more, indicated that they were alike in one point: The partners held certain deep spiritual convictions in common.

3. *This calls for an inexhaustible supply.*

(1) The psalmist speaks of an overflowing cup—"My cup runneth over" (Ps. 23).

(2) The superficial Christian has little to enjoy and little to give. Stuttering through his testimony, he has been likened to a cup half full pathetically trying to run over.

II. AN ADEQUATE SPIRITUAL OUTLET
"Freely give."

1. *The opportunities for spiritual sharing are unlimited.*

(1) A godly mother-in-law, Naomi, in a pagan setting, had so lived that her daughter-in-law clung to her. "Thy God [shall be] my God" (Ruth 1:16).

(2) A "little maid" in Syria had so lived, as a slave, in that foreign land, that the illustrious commanding general of the

Syrian armies followed her advice, and was healed of leprosy by the prophet of God (2 Kings 5:1-14).

(3) A concerned friend has opportunities to provide the needed prompting to the salvation of a soul.

A regular church attendant who did not realize his responsibility was in the habit of going directly to his pew without looking to the right or to the left. When the service was dismissed, he would hurry away without speaking to anyone. The pastor urged him to take time to exchange greetings and enjoy a bit of fellowship, and thus add a further blessing to his observance of the Lord's Day. His reply was prompt and emphatic: "I believe in attending to my own business!" But was he really attending to his own business? By no means! The divine pattern includes sharing, no less than receiving.

2. *The rewards are immeasurable.*

   (1) Spiritual sharing is healthful—a proven therapy for faltering Christians.

   (2) Spiritual sharing is fruitful and God-honoring (John 15:5, 8).

   (3) Spiritual sharing is joyful (John 15:11).

CONCLUSION

1. *The man who gets but never gives, may last for years but never lives.*

2. *The Sea of Galilee gives and lives.* It receives the sparkling waters of the River Jordan, and sustains life—fish splash in its waters, and birds sing in the trees along the shore. It passes the sparkling waters along to the south, where they flow into another sea—which has no outlet—the Dead Sea—in which nothing lives and from which neither beast nor fowl will drink.

3. *The dedicated believer fulfills his mission,* in the rhythm of the abundant life, as he "freely receives" and "freely gives."

30. Giving Christ His Due

Matthew 25:14-30

INTRODUCTION
" . . . mine own with interest" (vs. 27).

1. *This parable points to a day of reckoning—"* . . . mine own with interest" (v. 27)—*from which there is no escape.* This is the main thrust.

   "We must all appear before the judgment seat of Christ" (2 Cor. 5:10).

2. *It spells out two RESPONSIBILITIES which cannot be set aside.*

   The one is quite familiar; the other has rarely received the emphasis it deserves.

I. WE ARE RESPONSIBLE TO GOD FOR ALL THE KNOWLEDGE, POWERS, AND RESOURCES WE POSSESS.

1. *The world's need raises a strong presumption of such responsibility.*

   (1) The need for that which God's people alone can supply is great enough in God-favored America, with more gospel light than elsewhere.

   (2) The need is immeasurably greater in troubled areas of the world where suppression and violence prevail, and where unmet spiritual needs cry out to heaven.

   (3) It hardly needs to be argued that knowledge bears responsibility toward ignorance; strength toward weakness; wealth toward poverty.

   (4) It requires no elaborate interpretation to make plain the words of Jesus—"Unto whomsoever much is given . . . much [is] required" (Luke 12:48).

2. *The Word of God does not leave us with only a presumption of responsibility.* "As my Father hath sent me, even so send I you" (John 20:21)—not "to live and let live," but "to live and *help* live."

3. *The test of our devotion, how we relate ourselves to the will of Christ.* But, looking around us, what do we see?

   (1) Good people who do not carry their goodness into the weekdays.

   The superintendent of a certain Sunday school was far above average in giftedness and ability. The boys of his Sunday school knew him only as a warm, friendly, outgoing personality. But when two of them were engaged to keep his large lawn mowed, they were utterly unprepared to find him such a glum, uncommunicative person as he proved to be on weekdays. On Sundays he did indeed "adorn the doctrine of God" (Titus 2:10); he "let his light shine" (Matt. 5:16); but on weekdays there remained only a tiny glimmer of the light that shone so brightly on Sundays.

   (2) God does His work largely through limited, ungifted men and women, while ten-talented men and women fail to make themselves available.

   (3) Consecrated, overworked men and women are handicapped by sheer weariness.

II. WE ARE RESPONSIBLE TO GOD FOR ALL THE KNOWLEDGE, POWERS, AND RESOURCES WE OUGHT TO POSSESS.

1. *"I have not the knowledge" is the plea of many;* but—John 7:17.

   (1) How bitterly the author of Hebrews protests needless immaturity—Heb. 5:12!

   (2) How earnestly Paul appeals to his fellow-Christians to inform themselves! Six times he writes, "I would not have you ignorant, brethren" (Rom. 1:13; 11:25; 1 Cor. 10:1; 12:1; 2 Cor. 1:8; 1 Thess. 4:13

   (3) How solemnly Jesus warns against needless ignorance (Matt. 25:41-46)!

   An unusually friendly barber was giving a haircut to a new customer. By way of getting acquainted, he inquired into the background and vocation of the customer, who happened to be a Baptist minister. This opened the way for the minister to inquire into the spiritual interests of the barber. "Do you happen to be a Baptist also?" No, he did not belong to any church; he never attended any church; and never had, although there were dozens of churches in that city, with church bells ringing from many towers on Sunday mornings. "If you pass up these opportunities so completely, how will you ever justify this before the Lord, in the day of reckoning?" "No problem," said the barber, "the Lord will recognize at once that 'that poor, ignorant guy didn't know any better,' and so He won't be too hard on me." But salvation by ignorance is not in the plan of redemption!

2. *"I have not the powers," is the plea of others;* but no Christian is powerless when completely dedicated (Acts 1:8; 1 Tim. 4:14).

3. *"I have not the resources,"* is the plea of others; but, "Give ye them to eat," said the Lord Jesus, when there were only five loaves and two fishes for feeding the five thousand!

CONCLUSION

" . . . mine own with interest"—this is the measure of our responsibility to Christ.

1. *Every human possession and potential points to some divine purpose.*

2. *Every life becomes meaningful when we give Christ His due*—self, service, and substance—and come into the fullness of the abundant life (John 10:10).

31. The Marks of a Christian

Luke 5:1-11

INTRODUCTION

1. *The disciples were called Christians first in Antioch* (Acts 11:26).

   (1) The term implies qualities of life by which the pagan mind identified Christians with their acknowledged Lord.

   (2) The world is quick to discern and eager to stigmatize those who live the "separated life."

2. *The disciples were soon marked with more than the stigma of a name.*

   (1) Paul, sent from Antioch, declared: "I bear in my body the marks of the Lord Jesus" (Gal. 6:17); he was beaten, stoned, imprisoned (2 Cor. 11:23-25).

   (2) Early church fathers often came to their councils bruised, mutilated, scarred, but serene and joyful, like Paul.

3. *The disciples whom the world acknowledges with labels of derision and marks of violence are known to God by marks of the soul.*

   (1) Without these marks, the external graces for which men are praised have no merit with God—"The Lord looketh on the heart" (1 Sam. 16:7).

   (2) Without these *distinguishing MARKS of a Christian,* Peter would not have qualified on the memorable day:

I. AN ATTITUDE OF OBEDIENCE TO CHRIST
" . . . at thy word I will . . . " (v. 5).

1. *Peter responded in three distinct acts of obedience,* under the most trying circumstances.

   (1) Jesus appeared on shore when they had "toiled all night" and were washing their nets, and proposed a preaching service—untimely, yet Peter obeyed.

(2) Jesus proposed that they go fishing, when these seasoned fishermen had fished all night and caught nothing—yet Peter obeyed.

(3) Jesus proposed that they give up fishing and follow Him, as "fishers of men"—and Peter obeyed.

2. *Jesus made obedience a test of discipleship*—"Why call ye me Lord, Lord, and do not the things which I say" (Luke 6:46)?

(1) The difference between a disciple and others: "Thy will be done."

(2) The experience of the early disciples—"Lacked ye anything?" (Luke 22:35).

(3) The cost of discipleship is far below the cost of disobedience.

Two neighboring families appeared to be very much alike, but on Sundays there was a difference. From the one family the parents and six children made their way regularly to Sunday school and church services. From the other, there was only occasional attendance by only a part of the family. The father was urgently invited, but felt no need. He was "living a clean life, treating everybody right, and observing the Golden Rule." He was working hard to support the family and to pay off the mortgage on the home. "What more can you ask?" But fifteen years later, an inquiry revealed that the family had broken up, and the father had become "a broken old man," before his time—divorced, alone, brooding, and miserable (Ps. 127:1-2).

II. AN ATTITUDE OF DEVOTION TO CHRIST
"They forsook all, and followed Him" (v. 11).

1. *Devotion is the element which distinguishes the obedience of disciples from the obedience of devils.*

(1) Devils obey, but it is a cringing, sullen, reluctant obedience.

(2) Disciples obey out of love, not fear—"We love him because he first loved us" (1 John 4:19).

2. *Devotion is the saving quality which distinguishes the Christian faith from false religions.*

(1) How different from pagan sacrifices brought in fear to an unknown god!

(2) How different from the ritualistic prostrations of some religious cults!

On a distant continent we have seen, at the appointed time of prayer, individuals hurrying to the place of worship, with grim, tense, unhappy facial expression; they came out with the same grim, tense, unhappy facial expression—after going through all the prescribed prostrations and perfunctory prayers. In beautiful contrast, we see Susannah Wesley, the mother of the renowned John and Charles Wesley, at times retreating from the family scene when there was turbulence in that family of ten children—and returning moments later completely relaxed, and with an incomprehensible calmness, poise, and serenity. In the course of time the children came to understand the source of her strength—her devotional life and two-way communion with the Heavenly Father. "They that wait upon the Lord shall renew their strength" (Isa. 40:31), like refilling a cup from the inexhaustible waters of a higher altitude.

3. *Devotion keeps open the channel through which the finest qualities of soul are imparted.*

   (1) "If any man have not the Spirit of Christ, he is none of his" (Rom. 8:9).

   (2) "The fruit of the Spirit is love . . . " (Gal. 5:22).

   (3) "By their fruits ye shall know them" (Matt. 7:20).

4. *Devotion gives continuity to obedience.*

5. *Devotion to Christ is the bond which holds the church together.*

   Like the invisible cord holding a precious string of pearls together.

CONCLUSION

The responses of Peter are the marks of a true Christian.

1. Obedience was the essence of that first response to the Lord Jesus: " . . . at thy word I will. . . ."

2. Devotion was the essence of that last recorded conversation with Christ: " . . . thou knowest that I love thee . . . " (John 21:17).

32. Warnings from Gethsemane

Luke 22:31-34, 39-48, 54-62

INTRODUCTION

1. *The most important week in the earthly life of Jesus* was the week of His crucifixion and resurrection—"To this end was I born" (John 18:37).

2. *The darkest night—the night of Gethsemane.*

    (1) In the upper room He breaks bread, prefiguring His death; and foretells betrayal, denial, and desertion.

    (2) In the garden He prays alone; then the tumult, with soldiers advancing "with lanterns and torches and weapons" (John 18:3).

3. *The saddest moment—the denial by Peter.* How could he?

    (1) His life was clean (John 15:3); he had strength of character—"strengthen thy brethren" (Luke 22:32); he was devoted to his Master.

    (2) His failure and the *FACTORS in his fall* carry warnings to every heart:

I. OVER-CONFIDENCE IN SELF

1. *He had honestly purposed to be faithful* (v. 33; Matt. 26:35).

2. *He had forgotten the warning of Jesus*—"thou shalt deny . . . " (v. 34).

3. *He had forgotten how completely he was dependent on Christ*—"Lord, save me" (Matt. 14:30).

4. *He had not learned what Paul reflected after twenty years in the front lines:* "Who is sufficient? . . . our sufficiency is of God" (2 Cor. 2:16; 3:5).

II. PRAYERLESSNESS IN TIME OF DANGER

1. *"Pray that ye enter not into temptation"* (v. 40); yet they slept (v. 45).

2. *"Men ought always to pray"* (Luke 18:1).

   Be *always* alert and responsive to the voice of the Holy Spirit—not just at "prayer time." An elderly saint gave this interpretation: "When you have made the connection and have poured out your heart in a torrent of petition and intercession, don't hang up the receiver! Keep the line open!" This counsel agrees with the conclusion of the apostolic admonition to "put on the whole armour of God" (Eph. 6:11-18). Seven pieces of "armour" are enumerated—seven heavenly defenses for earthly living: the helmet of salvation, the breastplate of righteousness, the girdle of truth, the shield of faith, the sword of the Spirit, the gospel of peace, and the atmosphere of prayer. Significantly, the context suggests that when all the other pieces of "armour" are in place, let the whole of man be enveloped in the atmosphere of prayer.

3. *"Life is fragile; handle with prayer"*—Do not go unattended and unsheltered into the dangerous unknown.

   (1) Any day may be the turning point of a life.

   (2) A day prayerlessly begun may be spoiled and never fully retrieved.

III. BROKEN FELLOWSHIP

1. *Separated from Christ*—"Peter followed afar off" (v. 54).

2. *Separated from the brethren*—like Elijah, who broke down, thinking he was alone, although there were seven thousand other believers (1 Kings 19:14, 18).

   (1) "Woe to him that is alone when he falleth" (Eccles. 4:10).

   (2) "Consider one another . . . not forsaking the assembling . . . " (Heb. 10:24-25).

IV. EVIL ASSOCIATIONS

1. *"Peter sat down among them"* (v. 55).

   He found comfort and disaster by the devil's fire.

2. *"Blessed is the man that walketh not . . . standeth not . . . sitteth not . . . "* (Ps. 1). Peter did all three.

   A teen-ager in a Chicago suburb had gotten into serious trouble. When he was found guilty and the judge pronounced sentence upon him, the mother made a tearful, impassioned plea for his release. "He has always been such a good boy; he just got into bad company!" She was forgetting that when a good boy gets into bad company he ceases to be a good boy; likewise, a good girl ceases to be a good girl; and the same is true of a good man or a good woman. "Be not conformed to this world" (Rom. 12:2).

CONCLUSION

"Let him that thinketh he standeth take heed lest he fall" (1 Cor. 10:12).

1. The denial of Christ may take many forms.

   "The cruelest lies are often told in silence" (Robert Louis Stevenson).

2. The safeguards are ever the same.

   Humility, prayerfulness, Christian fellowship, and avoidance of evil associations.

33. Almost Too Good to Be Saved

John 3:1-7, 14-17

INTRODUCTION

1. *The spiritual biography of Nicodemus* is sketched in three widely separated Scriptural incidents.

   (1) One, alone with Jesus, in the night, about three months after the beginning of His ministry; one, with the Council, about two and a half years later; one, with Joseph of Arimathca, burying the body of Jesus.

   (2) Each incident gives evidence of spiritual progress: an honest inquirer; a timid defender; an acknowledged disciple.

2. *The moral excellence of Nicodemus* is implied in his honorable position.

   (1) As a teacher of religion, he represented the highest moral attainment.

   (2) As ruler and member of the Sanhedrin he was held in high esteem.

3. *His goodness and nearness to the Kingdom brought him to Jesus.*

4. *His goodness almost became his undoing,* in delaying his breakthrough.

   Three SPIRITUAL PORTRAITS, over a period of three years, tell the story:

I. AN HONEST INQUIRER   John 3:1-7, 14-17

1. *His coming to Jesus was prompted by honest concern.*

   (1) Honest with himself—knew he lacked something, willing to admit it, anxious to meet the deficiency.

   (2) Honest with those he taught—knew he could not give what he did not have.

   (3) Honest with Jesus—glad to acknowledge the truth about Jesus so far as it had been revealed to him (v. 2).

2. *His coming required a large measure of courage.*

   (1) True, he came by night—mentioned three times—but he *came,* despite formidable barriers.

   (2) True, he feared the Jews, but with reason, especially after the cleansing of the temple (John 2:13-16).

3. *His coming was not in vain.*

   Jesus gave him "the Bible in miniature" (v. 16), and the key to entrance into the Kingdom (v. 7).

II. A TIMID DEFENDER—John 7:44-53

1. *Was he still groping toward spiritual reality and certainty*—after two and one-half years?

2. *Had he become a true disciple,* but without the courage to let it be known?

   (1) He had certainly made some spiritual progress, reflected in his question.

   (2) But he was silent when he might have borne testimony— "Have any of the rulers or Pharisees believed . . . " (v. 48)?

III. AN ACKNOWLEDGED DISCIPLE—John 19:38-42

1. *Events had moved rapidly since that meeting of the Pharisees* six months before.

   (1) The wrath of the Pharisees and chief priests had increased in bitterness and fury; Jesus was crucified, with the mob howling its approval.

   (2) The cause of Christ had apparently collapsed; Judas had betrayed his Lord; Peter had denied Him; the disciples were scattered.

2. *Two men come and boldly identify themselves with the crucified Christ.*

   (1) Something has happened—two members of the Supreme Court tenderly lay away the body of Jesus, at their own peril.

   (2) Something has at last become clear to Nicodemus: to be interested is not enough (John 3:1, 2); to be favorably disposed is not enough (John 7:50-51); nothing short of total commitment will suffice.

CONCLUSION

1. *The story of Nicodemus is constantly being reenacted.*

   A middle-aged school teacher, with all the external graces of clean living and high standards, could see no reason for becoming a Christian. But a devout neighbor who was afraid to go out alone on Sunday evenings persuaded her to come along. After attending a number of services with her friend, she apologized to the pastor for being in the services. She felt like a hypocrite sitting in the pew and listening to preaching that she could not accept. She emphasized that she was present only because of her neighbor's insistence. Months later, in conversation with the pastor, she ridiculed the practice of inviting people to walk down the aisle and present themselves for baptism and church membership. Her rejection of everything about the church was as emphatic as ever. But after about a year the pastor found a note in his mail box: "I'm ready now—for baptism, and all that it involves." After this, her first concern was for the unenlisted mothers of children in the Sunday school; and she became instrumental in building up a substantial class composed of such mothers. Such is the blessed fruitage of continuing under the illumination, stimulation, and discipline of the Word of God.

2. *The story of Nicodemus is a warning against the illusions of secret discipleship.*

   "Whosoever shall confess me before men, him will I confess . . . " (Matt. 10:32). But there is no such promise to "secret disciples." And there is every reason to doubt the salvation of Nicodemus until his open identification of himself with the crucified Christ. Thus there are many good people who are "not far from the kingdom," but still definitely outside. One indispensable step remains to be taken before salvation of the soul becomes a reality, coupled with the "peace of God" and the blessed assurance of "everlasting life."

34. The Key to All Blessings

John 7:14-18; 8:31-32

INTRODUCTION

1. *There are a thousand roadblocks along the way to heaven,* but only one that can keep a soul out: the unwillingness to render obedience and allegiance to Him who is "the way, the truth, and the life" (John 14:6). It is the attitude that says, "I will not." Jesus wept over those who *"would not"* (Luke 13:34).

2. *There are a thousand devices with which men have sought to enter heaven,* but there is only one way to open the door: the response that says, "Lord, what wilt thou have me to do?" (Acts 9:6).

This willingness is the key to all our *BLESSINGS:*

I. THE KEY TO OUR SALVATION—John 7:17

1. *The willing soul realizes he is a created being* (Ps. 100:3) in a created world that is moving toward the goal of creation.

    The unwilling soul insists on being his own god, and seeks to master the universe for his own glory (Gen. 11:4).

2. *The willing soul asks, how can I fit my life into the plan of my Creator?*

    The unwilling soul ignores the Creator, like an employee who ignores his employer, works hard, wonders why there is no raise, no praise, no promotion.

3. *The willing soul, hearing a voice in the night, responds, like Samuel* (1 Sam. 3:10).

    The unwilling soul hears no such voice. God does not speak to unwilling ears, or reveal Himself to unwilling eyes, or come with salvation and blessing into an unwilling heart.

4. *The willing soul prays, "Thy will be done," and tries to conform.*

    The unwilling soul may pray, in effect, *"My* will be done, with God's help"; but "even his prayer is an abomination" to God (Prov. 28:9).

    A young woman who had been preparing for vocational Christian service discovered that she was one of those "almost Chris-

tians." Her lifestyle was above reproach, she was active in church, and she enjoyed the thrill of leadership; but she was fashioning her own career instead of submitting to the Lord. An illness brought her to the greatest turning point in her life. Unaccustomed to illness, she sank into a spirit of despondency, with feelings of worthlessness, helplessness, and hopelessness. Finally, in utter despair, she threw up her hands and prayed, "Lord, I'm through! You take over!" Instead of sinking deeper, she experienced such a sense of peace as she had never known. Life has never been the same since that moment when, in a real sense, Christ became the Lord of her life.

II. THE KEY TO ALL FURTHER BLESSING—
Prov. 3:6; 4:18

1. *The promise of Jesus* is conditional: "If ye continue in my word ..." (John 8:31-32).

2. *The experience of Saul:* Without compliance he might have remained blind (Acts 9:6).

3. *The counsel to "Pilgrim,"* fleeing from the City of Destruction to the Celestial City: "Keep that light in your eyes, and go directly to it" (*Pilgrim's Progress*).

4. *The changeless formula by which "God leads His dear children along":*

   (1) A road map (Ps. 37:23), with a lighted path (Ps. 119:105).

   (2) A personal Guide—The Holy Spirit "will guide you into all truth" (John 16:13).

   (3) The help of providential opening and closing of doors (Acts 16:6-12).

III. THE KEY TO OUR HEAVENLY HOME

1. *Guiding the soul to the Haven of Rest, are three "harbor lights."*

   A passenger on a small ship crossing the English Channel on a dark night was wondering how, in that remote area, the pilot would ever find his way into the harbor. The pilot explained: "No problem at all. Do you see those three lights in the far distance? As we move along the shore we will reach a point from which the three lights will be in a straight line, one above the other, leading directly into the harbor." Such is the threefold guidance of the Scriptures, providential circumstances, and the promptings of the Holy Spirit.

2. *Opening the door to the heavenly home, calls only for continuing movement* in the right direction, like opening the door of the supermarket.

3. *Awaiting the pilgrim at his homecoming is the heavenly family.* Who? (Rev. 7:13-14).

   (1) "As many as are led by the Spirit of God . . . " (Rom. 8:14, 17).

   (2) "Whosoever shall do the will of my Father . . . " (Matt. 12:48, 50).

   (3) A select company—reconciled, cleansed, transformed! (1 John 1:9; 3:2). But "not every one shall enter . . . " (Matt. 7:21).

   A woman with three churches in her immediate neighborhood never found it convenient to concern herself about spiritual things. When she died, her loved ones wanted her to have "a decent Christian burial." They made arrangements with the nearest pastor, who endeavored to be helpful. It was a difficult assignment, and in the service there was one surprise for which he was utterly unprepared. Arrangements had been made with the church soloist to sing, by request of the family, "Beautiful Isle of Somewhere"! No, there is no "beautiful isle of somewhere" for the unwilling. All the promises are to "whosoever will"; none to "whosoever won't."

CONCLUSION

1. *The standing invitation to forgiveness and cleansing* runs through the Holy Scripture like a golden thread: "Come . . . " (Isa. 1:18).

2. *The last call to reconciliation* is in the very last chapter: "Come . . . " (Rev. 22:17).

3. *The blessedness of full commitment* is reflected by the apostle Paul in his last Epistle: "I know . . . " (2 Tim. 1:12).

35. The Other Sheep

John 10:1-5, 9-16

INTRODUCTION

This Scripture passage presents Jesus in two highly significant figures of speech.

1. *In the first analogy Jesus is the "door" to the "sheepfold," a* symbol of the church.

   (1) There are other ways to come in—usually no trickery or willful deception, but want of understanding.

   (2) Those coming in by other ways are a threat to the peace and security of the "fold."

   (3) Those coming in by the "door" shall be "saved."

2. *In the second analogy Jesus is the "shepherd" of the sheep.*

   (1) The true shepherd knows his sheep, calls them by name, "leads them out."

   (2) The true sheep knows the voice of the shepherd.

   The newborn lamb soon recognizes its own mother's bleat among that of a thousand others. For the understanding of a sheep, it is necessary to be born a sheep; for the eyes of an eagle . . . born an eagle; for the understanding of a child of God . . . "born again."

   (3) The true believer, like the true sheep, follows his "Shepherd" (Ps. 23).

   The "unsaved" can not recite, with sincerity, the 23rd Psalm. The Lord is not his "Shepherd"; he has never accepted that relationship. The true sheep looks to his shepherd, and follows. But the untamed, long-horned steer on the western prairie does not follow the cowboy to the corral; instead, he tears away in the opposite direction. The cowboy, on a speedy and powerful horse, overtakes him and throws the rope, bringing him to a violent fall. Then, dragging the steer by the neck, he brings him—still resistant, struggling, puffing, sweating, and exhausted—into the corral. The "unsaved" would need to paraphrase the 23rd Psalm and say, *"The Lord is my* cowboy; *that is why I am having such a hard time."*

(4) The "Good Shepherd," with infallible discernment, "knoweth them that are his" (2 Tim. 2:19).

3. *In the concluding verse (v. 16), are two implied INVITATIONS to cooperate with the "Good Shepherd":*

I. AN INVITATION TO "FOLLOWERS" TO SHARE THE SAVIOR'S CONCERN FOR THE "OTHER SHEEP"

1. *Sheep, so called in anticipation, by divine foreknowledge* (Rom. 8:29; Acts 18:10).

(1) Seekers after truth and grace, like buds ready to bloom: "Certain Greeks" (John 12:20, 21); Ethiopian (Acts 8:26-28); Lydia (Acts 16:14-15).

(2) Willful resisters to truth and grace: the mob on Calvary (Mark 15:29-30; Acts 2:37); Saul of Tarsus (Acts 9:1-6).

(3) Sinners all around us, whose salvation depends on concern of "followers."

(4) People beyond the homeland, in many fields.

2. *Sheep differing in race, language, nationality.*

(1) Jesus, disregarding traditional barriers, included all (Matt. 8:11).

(2) Unbelieving Jews did not conceal their resentment of this inclusiveness.

(3) True disciples rejoice, reveal nearness to Christ by sharing His concern.
Test of Peter's devotion: "lovest thou me . . . feed my sheep" (John 21:16).
Test of dating partner: "Love me . . . love my dog!"
Proof of salvation: concern for salvation of others.

II. AN INVITATION TO "OTHER SHEEP" TO SHARE THE SAVIOR'S CONCERN FOR HIS OWN SALVATION

1. *Without the love of God and the concern of others, none would be saved.*

(1) God the Father "so loved" that He gave His Son (John 3:16; Jer. 31:3).

(2) God the Son "so loved" that He came "to seek and to save" (Luke 19:10).

(3) God the Holy Spirit "so loved" that He never ceased warning and calling.

(4) Angels of God are concerned (Heb. 1:14; Luke 15:10).

(5) Friends in heaven and on earth are concerned (2 Cor. 5:20).

2. *Without a corresponding concern on the part of the "other sheep" all is vain.*

The front page of a big city newspaper carried a startling picture of a man falling from an upper window of a tall skyscraper. This man, in a moment of dark despair, had climbed out the window to leap to his death. Then he hesitated for a long time on the broad ledge outside the window. When he was seen, there was tremendous excitement. He was just beyond physical reach from inside the window. Every effort of persuasion was fruitless. A vast crowd gathered on the street below. Many were begging him to reenter the window; many were praying, "Lord, save him!" But all was in vain; he made the leap and crashed to his death on the pavement below. He himself cast the deciding vote. Ultimately, the destiny of the "other sheep" depends on his own response to the "Good Shepherd."

CONCLUSION

The words of the Savior (v. 16) carry a message to every heart.

1. To the "follower"—share your faith—"Freely ye have received, freely give" (Matt. 10:8).

2. To the "other sheep"—"Come unto me . . . " (Matt. 11:28-30; John 6:37).

3. To all alike—"My Spirit shall not always strive with man" (Gen. 6:3); time is running out!

36. The Lord's Breakfast

John 21:1-15

INTRODUCTION

1. *The seven discouraged apostles with whom Jesus reestablished contact* by the Sea of Galilee must have been hungry with a threefold hunger:

    (1) Physical hunger, after a long night of strenuous toil.

    (2) Emotional hunger, from prolonged frustration and failure.

    (3) Spiritual hunger, which separation from Christ produces.

2. *The Lord's Breakfast, which satisfied all hunger,* must have been one of the most heartwarming experiences of their lives.

    (1) How vividly they remembered the last previous meal with their Lord in the blessed togetherness of that upper room!

    (2) How empty their lives had been without His presence!

    (3) How wonderful His return to their midst!

    (4) How comforting the ASSURANCES which came with the restoration of that fellowship:

I. HIS CONCERN FOR EVERY DRIFTING DISCIPLE

1. *He does not give us up when we become unfaithful.*

   A barber in a distant city had just given me an exceptionally careful haircut. As I expressed my appreciation, he surprised me with this reply: "I'm getting out of this business just as soon as I can find other work. I do my best for every customer, and I take pride in my work; but when I am pleased with the result, and my customer goes away happy, that is not the end. The next time he comes in, he looks as shabby as ever; and I have to start all over again. The frustration of it all is getting me down. I just can't take it any longer!" One of the most amazing attributes of the Savior is His patience with us, and His readiness to cleanse and forgive, again and again. The pastor, facing his church family on Sundays, finds it sobering indeed to see persons with burdens and heartaches of which perhaps only the pastor is aware; but how thrilling to note the presence of dedicated persons who had drifted but had been restored and "warmed over," like those seven apostles by the Sea of Galilee!

2. *He showed concern for Peter, who had so shamefully denied Him* (Mark 14:72).

   (1) On the morning of His resurrection, He sent word—"Tell Peter . . . " (Mark 16:7).

   (2) On the same day He personally appeared to Peter (Luke 24:34).

3. *He followed the disciples to the Sea of Galilee*—"the Good Shepherd" (John 10:14).

4. *He sends message after message,* through appointed messengers, disciplines, and promptings of the conscience.

II. HIS POWER TO SAVE FROM FAILURE

1. *He had told them, "Without me ye can do nothing"* (John 15:5). Now they knew it!

   (1) Fishing on the wrong side of the boat, till Jesus came (John 21:6).

   (2) Building a good life, a happy home, a "Great Society," is impossible without Him.

   Apart from Christ, one might "gain the whole world, and lose his own soul" (Mark 8:36), or live in destitution, and "lose his own soul." Many a destitute person might have his need supplied through Christ, and many a millionaire might be saved from the curse of forbidden wealth. The windmill, upon which the western plainsmen depend for water, operates best with a moderate breeze. A breeze brings water; a tempest destroys the mill. The breeze of divine favor brings endless blessing; the alternative is "leanness of soul" (Ps. 106:15), an emptiness that material abundance cannot fill. A recent story in the news media told of a young man who was deeply absorbed in making a fortune, and succeeded in becoming a multimillionaire before the prime of life. But the cost was too great. Separated from his family, and feeling a great emptiness in his life, he declared, "If I had my life to live over again, I'd ask God to take the ambition out of me."

2. *He came not to deprive, but to enrich; not to limit, but to enlarge* (John 10:10).

(1) All legitimate enterprise is more productive with His help (Ps. 1; 1 Tim. 4:8).

(2) All "your *need*" shall be supplied "by Christ Jesus" (Phil. 4:19; Matt. 6:33).

III. HIS ABILITY TO PROVIDE FOR HIS OWN

1. *With His own hands, He prepared breakfast and fed the disciples*—"Come and dine."

2. *With His hidden helpers everywhere, needs were never unmet:*

   Fish for that breakfast; a coin (Matt. 17:27); a boat (Luke 5:3); a beast of burden (Mark 11:2); an upper room (Mark 14:15); a prepared sepulchre (John 19:41-42).

3. *With His own resources, He feeds the world* (Ps. 145:15).

IV. HIS LONGING TO REINSTATE EVERY DRIFTING DISCIPLE

1. *A heart hunger corresponding to their own, bringing Him to the Sea of Galilee.*

2. *A longing like that of the father of the Prodigal Son* (Luke 15:20).

3. *A readiness to forgive, heal the breach, restore the fellowship.*

   (1) A spirit out of adjustment is like a bone out of joint: no salve, no medication, no psychotherapy will do—nothing but adjustment of the parts.

   (2) A conscience burning with remorse cries for forgiveness— nothing less!

CONCLUSION

1. *Like the Lord's Breakfast,* the Lord's Supper is designed to meet the soul's deepest hunger—"Come and dine."

2. *Like Peter, arising from the Lord's Breakfast*—"forgiven, restored, renewed in devotion—let every believer respond, "My Jesus, I love Thee. . . ."

37. Venturing into the Unknown (New Year.)

Joshua 3:1-7

INTRODUCTION

1. *At last, after 430 years in bondage and 40 years in the wilderness, Israel is ready to cross over into Canaan.*

   (1) A land "flowing with milk and honey," but separated from them by the bridgeless, turbulent, swollen River Jordan.

   (2) A land peopled with giants, in fortified cities, bristling with preparations for their destruction.

   (3) A land of mystery, peril, and promise—Joshua counsels faith and courage.

2. *Like Israel, we are venturing into the unknown, as the new year dawns.*

   (1) "Oh, for a bit of omniscience!" No, thank God, we do not know what the future holds!

   (2) "Give me light to enter the dark unknown!" "No, put your hand in His hand; that is better than light, and safer than a known way."

   (3) Give heed to the heaven-sent DIRECTIVES which guided Israel over the Jordan, and which are equally appropriate for us:

I. FOLLOW THE ARK
"When ye see the ark . . .
the priests bearing it . . . go after it" (v. 3).

1. *A sacred treasure chest,* a portable shrine, 4 by 2½ by 2½ feet, gold covered, containing the stone "tables" of the law, and Aaron's rod, and a manna pot.

2. *A symbol of God's presence, guiding them.* Thus assured, the soul is fortified.

Similarly, the legacy of Jesus—the concluding assurance of the Great Commission—looms large.

A missionary couple on furlough gave a deeply moving account of their first term of service in the remote hills of Burma. Leaving home, they had traveled first by airplane; then by ocean liner across the seas; then on foreign soil by train; then over many miles of rough road by jeep; and finally on foot, along a lonely, dimly marked path winding through the jungle. Again and again, they drooped in discouragement. But each time their spirits revived with remembrance of the blessed assurance that they were not walking alone, but with the Lord who had called them. With the lift of this assurance, their missionary service was happy and fruitful; and they were eagerly looking forward to their return to the field.

3. *A memorial, reminding them of the past faithfulness of God—*their deliverance, the manna, the mercy seat.

4. *A promise of gracious providences to come—*"As I was with Moses, so will I be with thee."

   (1) There will be changes, but not in "the grand continuity of the grace of God."

   (2) There may be disappointments, disciplines, injuries, losses, and sufferings; but "all things work together for good to them that love God" (Rom. 8:28).

II. PROCEED WITH CAUTION

1. *"There shall be a space between you and it . . . "* (v. 4).

   Let there be patience—no pellmell rush, no scramble, no impulsive moves; but thoughtful, watchful observance of the guidelines.

2. *"Ye have not passed this way heretofore"* (v. 4).

   They had learned much, but could not learn enough in ten thousand years to walk alone.

3. *You will not pass this way again.*

   Our paths are like footprints in soft concrete—they cannot be erased.

III. SANCTIFY YOURSELVES (v. 5).

1. *A time for spiritual inventory.*

   Check spiritual growth, progress, altitude, temperature, assets, liabilities.

2. *A time for spiritual adjustments.*

   Perhaps a belated spiritual housecleaning, with repentance, confession, reconciliation, restitution, and payment of unkept vows (Matt. 5:23-24; 18:15-16).

3. *A time for thanksgiving.*

   For common blessings; happy memories; disciplines (wisely conceived, not relished, but profitable to the soul); nightmares that never came true; punishments not received (Ps. 103:10; Lam. 3:22).

4. *A time for godly resolutions.*

   Give heed to every holy prompting; be concrete; observe the rules for establishing good habits.

CONCLUSION

1. *The first rainbow of which we have any record* is the rainbow that appeared to Noah and his family after they emerged from the ark. They made their new beginning in a true spirit of worship, with an altar and sacrifices "unto the Lord" (Gen. 8:20); and God responded with rich promises, of which the rainbow was to be a perpetual reminder (Gen. 8:22; 9:13). To them and to every later generation of believers it carries the same blessed assurance: above the clouds, the sun is shining; and a loving Heavenly Father is watching over His own (Gen. 8:12-16).

2. *The first words of the first Gospel message* were the words, "Fear not," proclaimed by the angel preacher in the hills of Bethlehem the night when the Savior was born. How appropriate that the observance of Christmas should come just before the beginning of the new year! And how appropriate that there should be 365 "Fear nots" in the Holy Scriptures (addressed to believers)—a fresh "Fear not" for every day in the year!

3. *The first concern of all who are privileged to begin a new year* should be to "examine yourselves ... " (2 Cor. 13:5); then "acknowledge him, and he shall direct thy paths" (Prov. 3:6).

38. Singing in Jerusalem
(Palm Sunday)

Luke 19:29-40

INTRODUCTION

1. *Never before was Christ so spectacular as on that "Palm Sunday."*

    (1) He had come to Jerusalem to die—determined that Jerusalem should know.

    "The city was stirred . . . who is this" (Matt. 21:10, ASV)?

    (2) He died with the eyes of Jerusalem upon Him.

    Cross on sky line, darkness, earthquake, veil rent in temple.

2. *Never was the commonplace more beautifully devoted to His honor.*

    (1) The palms were made to praise Him; heaven was in that Hosanna chorus.

    (2) The multitude was acknowledging His Lordship, of which there are several *REFLECTIONS in this incident:*

I. HE HAS FULL KNOWLEDGE OF HIS RESOURCES
" . . . ye shall find a colt . . . " (v. 30).

1. *The colt—yes, it was His—*"every beast . . . and the cattle upon a thousand hills" (Ps. 50:10).

2. *The fish in the depth of the sea—*bringing up a coin from the unseen treasury of God (Matt. 17:27).

3. *The wealth in human hands—*"the silver is mine, and the gold . . . " (Hag. 2:8); "the tithe," whether gratefully offered or grudgingly withheld (Lev. 27:30).

    In the preamble of a marriage service, the minister, who was the father of the bride, remarked that he could not think of any-thing new to say to his daughter. But he felt impelled to call attention once more to the four pillars upon which a truly happy home must be built: The Lord's Day—"Remember the sabbath day, to keep it holy" (Exod. 20:8); the Lord's tithe—"The tithe is the Lord's" (Lev. 27:30); the family altar (Deut. 11:18-21); and the family pew (Heb. 10:25). Faithfulness in these areas of stewardship is never unnoticed, unremembered, or unrewarded by the Heavenly Father.

II. HE DESIGNS THAT ALL HIS EARTHLY RESOURCES SHOULD SERVE HIM
" . . . loose him, and bring him . . . " (v. 30).

1. *Resources in the hands of friends—no problem.*

When needed, a boat was available (Luke 5:3); likewise, an "upper room" (Luke 22:12); and even a prepared sepulcher, a hundred yards from the place of His crucifixion (John 19:41).

2. *Resources in the hands of enemies—no less real.*

Somewhere a woodsman had prepared a cross; a teamster with his oxen had hauled it to the city; a leather worker had prepared the thongs for the scourging; a sluggard had allowed the thorns to grow, for the crown of thorns; a blacksmith had forged the nails; and an artisan had fashioned a spear to pierce His side.

3. *Resources actual and potential.*

The disciples, facing a hungry multitude of five thousand, with only five loaves and two fishes, were bidden, "Give ye them to eat" (Luke 9:13).

The parable of the irresponsible steward emphasizes responsibility for the potential as well as the actual (Matt. 25:27).

III. HE ENTRUSTS TO MAN THE ADMINISTRATION OF HIS EARTHLY RESOURCES
" . . . the Lord hath need of him" (v. 31).

1. *The owner had it in his power to "loose the colt," or to refuse.*

2. *The owner set loose the greatest Hosanna chorus since the birth of Christ* (Luke 2:13-14).

3. *The believer must hear again that sovereign voice—"Loose him . . . " (v. 30).*

(1) If Jesus came to our city this Palm Sunday, would it be a triumphal entry?

(2) If Jesus came, would our spiritual state move Him to tears (v. 41)?

CONCLUSION

1. *It was a great day in old Jerusalem when the multitude burst into singing*—but there was no singing until someone had "loosed the colt."

2. *It was a great day in the life of that apathetic, decadent church* on the western plains when revival came, and swept the community.

   For years, the services had languished, the property had deteriorated, and it became clear that something drastic had to be done if the church was to survive. Someone had a vision, and after a while the vision took hold. It was a reasonably prosperous area of farmers and ranchers, but the people had never really learned to give. Now the need was desperate, and people began to give—many of them, sacrificially. At last, with much rejoicing, the new church was dedicated. Shortly thereafter, a series of special meetings was held; and it was not surprising to learn that the church had experienced such a revival as had never been known in all that area. But nothing had happened until the members had "loosed the colt!"

3. *It is a great day in the life of every believer who has been holding out,* when he "looses the colt," and the abundant life begins (John 10:10).

39. Conscience at the Foot of the Cross (*Good Friday*)

Matthew 27:35-54

INTRODUCTION

1. *Of all the impressive portrayals of Christ in the Gospels,* the one that stands supreme and looms largest is the Christ of the cross.

    (1) This does not detract from the Biblical portrayal of the majestic Christ, commanding the sea, raising the dead, casting out devils; or the fearless Christ, with complete foreknowledge of the crucifixion, going to Jerusalem to meet His appointment with death; or the compassionate Christ, entering into the sorrows and sufferings of humanity, bending over the sick, weeping over the lost.

    (2) This is how John the Baptist introduced Jesus. "Behold the Lamb of God, which taketh away the sin of the world" (John 1:29).

2. *Of all the gripping events in the life of Christ,* none can compare in importance with the events of that last week, culminating in His crucifixion and resurrection.

    (1) So important are these events that the Gospel writers devote one third of the total record to this one week, which comprised only one seventeen-hundredth of the earthly life-span of Christ.

    (2) The most important single event in the life of Christ was His death, coupled with His resurrection from the dead.

3. *Of all the crucifixions that have stirred the souls of men,* none is comparable to the crucifixion of Christ.

    (1) This crucifixion fell into a pattern long familiar to that troubled generation.

    (2) This crucifixion might have seemed like just another familiar chore for the centurion. He was probably a seasoned soldier, a war-hardened, battle-tested veteran, who had witnessed and experienced and inflicted much cruelty.

    (3) This crucifixion was different. What were these *DIFFER-*

ENCES, which brought such fear and conviction to this calloused centurion, and the outcry, "Truly this was the Son of God" (Matt. 27:54)?

I. THE UNIQUE BEHAVIOR OF THAT MAN ON THE MIDDLE CROSS

1. *His likeness was the likeness of men, but His behavior and attributes were the behavior and attributes of Deity.*

2. *His poise was the poise not of a mere man, but of Deity.*

    (1) "He shall not strive, nor cry . . . in the streets" (Matt. 12:19; Isa. 42:2).

    (2) He reflects always that same quiet consciousness of power, calm assurance of control, clear sense of direction (John 18:37).

3. *His fearlessness was not the fearlessness of ignorance or recklessness,* but of complete trust and dedication (Ps. 27:1).

4. *His grace was not the grace of man, but of Deity.* For His crucifiers, whom He could have slain with one breath, He prays, "Father, forgive them, for they know not what they do" (Luke 23:34).

II. THE AWE-INSPIRING MIRACLES WHICH ATTENDED THIS CRUCIFIXION

1. *Total darkness at midday* (Matt. 27:45).

    As though the heavens could not bear to look upon the agonies and indignities inflicted upon the Son of God, the sun draped itself in total darkness.

2. *Terrifying earthquake* (Matt. 27:51).

    As though the earth could not bear to receive the blood drops of the Son of God, but was seized with convulsions of horror, the earth shook with a mighty earthquake.

3. *Rending of the veil in the temple* "from the top to the bottom" (Matt. 27:51).

    What could be more beautifully symbolic of the coming of heaven to earth, opening to sinners the way of access to the mercy seat!

III. THE UNPRECEDENTED STIRRINGS OF THE
CENTURION'S OWN CONSCIENCE

1. *The centurion's work was done.* The last words from the cross had been spoken. The quivering body on that middle cross had become still. The Savior of the world was dead! But "behind the dim unknown standeth God within the shadows, holding watch above His own."

2. *The centurion hears the voice of God.*

   (1) It penetrates the hardest heart, with the thickest crust, which none other can enter.

   A clever inventor is said to have devised a new kind of lock for an iron safe. Instead of the usual knob and dial, the only thing visible on the outside was a mouthpiece from an old-fashioned telephone. In the inner mechanism there was a tiny phonographic cylinder upon which a secret password was inscribed. When the project was completed, the builder challenged his fellow-technicians to open the safe. With their knowledge and experience, it was their boast that they could open any ordinary safe, whether given the combination or not. When they had tried in vain to open the new safe, and admitted their failure, the builder astounded them with the simplicity of the solution. He placed his lips close to the mouthpiece, and—in a clear, strong voice—enunciated the password. Instantly there was heard an almost inaudible click in the inner mechanism, and one of the technicians needed only to pull the handle, and the door was open! Such is the unique access of the Creator to the heart of every creature.

   (2) It speaks to every soul, even that of a small child.

   (3) It pursues the guilty to the ends of the earth (Ps. 139:7, 12).

CONCLUSION

1. *It was "at the cross" that they first saw the light—*this cross section of humanity.

   (1) The centurion, having witnessed all, cries out, "Truly this was the Son of God!"

   (2) The wicked thief on the cross, pleads, "Lord, remember me when thou comest into thy kingdom!" (Luke 23:42).

(3) "The people that came together to that sight . . . smote their breasts and returned" (Luke 23:48). Moments earlier they were a howling mob; now, silenced, terrified, conscience stricken, they went away not gloating in triumph, but smiting their breasts. With such a shattering preparation for Pentecost, no wonder that so many of those who had cried "crucify Him" were now anxiously asking, " . . . what shall we do?" (Acts 2:37).

2. *It is "at the cross" that we recognize afresh the voice of God* through conscience calling for response.

40. Good News from the Grave
(Easter)

Matthew 28:1-10

INTRODUCTION

1. *The first Gospel sermon was preached, near Bethlehem, the night Jesus was born.*

   An angel preacher, schooled in the throne room of heaven, brought the message, in 57 words—"I bring you good tidings . . . " (Luke 2:10).

2. *The first Easter proclamation was likewise communicated by an angel* (v. 5).

   (1) Same angel who spoke to Mary? (Luke 1:30); and to the shepherds? (Luke 2:10).

   (2) Same salutation: "Fear not . . . good tidings . . . "

3. *Earth's darkest night: body of Jesus in tomb—grief, remorse, despair.*

4. *Earth's brightest sunrise: Jesus emerging from tomb, triumphant over death.*

   What did the resurrection of Jesus mean to those who came within its radiance?

   What does it mean to us? It carries the assurance of three *HEAVENLY BENEFITS:*

I. COMFORT FOR THE SORROWING

They came "to see the sepulchre" and "departed with great joy" (v. 1, 8).

1. *Three grief-stricken women came "very early"* (Mark 16:1-2).

   (1) They came with anxiety—"Who shall roll away the stone?" (Mark 16:3).

   (2) They heard the angel: "Fear not! He is risen! Come and see! Go and tell!"

2. *Mary Magdalene returns alone; lingers in garden; is the first to see the risen Christ* (John 20:15).

3. *Jesus had said: "Because I live, ye shall live also"* (John 14:19).

(1) Death is not the end of life—only an incident along the way of everlasting life (John 3:36).

(2) "Comfort one another with these words" (1 Thess. 4:18).

Comfort for sorrow is beautifully expressed in one of our old familiar folk songs, "Old Black Joe." It stands in sharp contrast with that other song from the Old South, "My Old Kentucky Home": "The day goes by like a shadow o'er the heart . . . the time . . . to part; then . . . good night!" No prospect of another sunrise or anything better beyond! How different from the glory which "Old Black Joe" sees beyond! "Gone are my friends . . . from this world to a better land I know . . . I hear those gentle voices calling old black Joe . . . I'm coming, I'm coming!" Such is the blessed assurance of the believer.

II. HOPE FOR THE HOPELESS
" . . . we had hoped . . . " (Luke 24:21).

1. *Two despondent pedestrians were trudging wearily homeward,* to Emmaus, seven miles away, on that Sunday afternoon.

"One of them . . . was Cleopas" (Luke 24:18). The other, though not identified, is presumed to have been his wife. And the place in Emmaus where Jesus turned in for the evening meal with them (Luke 24:29-31) is presumed to have been their home. It is not clear whether the wife of this Cleopas was the same person as "the wife of Cleophas" (John 19:25), who was one of the women who had stood by the cross upon which the Savior died. In any event, the two persons who invited this stranger—"abide with us" (Luke 24:29)—must have been rather close to the ministry of Jesus, to have recognized Him in His breaking of the bread. And if one of them was indeed "the wife of Cleophas" who had witnessed the crucifixion of Christ, this would emphasize their despondency in reliving the shattering events of that black Friday (Luke 24:14).

2. *A mysterious stranger falls in step with them* (Luke 24:15).

(1) At first they could not understand why His presence brought such comfort.

(2) Then, another miracle: no longer exhausted, they hasten back to Jerusalem to tell "the eleven"; and there they see Jesus again (Luke 24:33, 36).

III. GRACE FOR THE GUILTY
"Tell his disciples and Peter . . . " (Mark 16:7).
"The Lord is risen indeed, and hath appeared to Simon"
(Luke 24:34).

1. *Peter, at the trial of Jesus, had shamefully denied his Lord.*

   (1) Jesus looked at Peter, and "Peter went out and wept bitterly" (Luke 22:62).

   On that sad, silent Saturday, was he remembering the words of Jesus, "Whosoever shall deny me before men . . . " (Matt. 10:32-33)?

   (2) Jesus sends word by the angel at the tomb: "Tell his disciples *and Peter*" (Mark 16:7); later on the same day Christ personally appeared to Peter (Luke 24:34).

   (3) Jesus, by the Sea of Galilee, restores him to his apostleship (John 21:15-17).

2. *Members of the mob that clamored for the crucifixion,* then witnessed the miracles of the cross, and went away remorsefully smiting their breasts (Luke 23:48), found grace, at Pentecost (Acts 2:37, 41). And who was the preacher? None other than Peter!

CONCLUSION

What is the meaning of Easter to our generation?

1. A heavenly response to the fears and tears of mankind—comfort for the sorrowing, hope for the hopeless, grace for the guilty.

2. A Hallelujah in the heart of the believer.

3. An invitation to others to make this a "personal Easter."

41. How Revivals Begin
(Pentecost)

Acts 2:1-4, 22-24, 37-47

INTRODUCTION

1. *A recurring need in every church is the need for a heaven-sent revival.*

   A revival to pass through the flock like a purifying flame, removing practices, thoughts, and attitudes that hinder the Holy Spirit.

   A revival to weld the church family together in one united, pure-hearted, clean-handed spiritual brotherhood.

   A revival to bring spiritual enrichment to the church family, and salvation to friends and loved ones.

2. *Our incomparable ideal is the revival of the first church in old Jerusalem.*

   (1) They had purity of doctrine—not enough; able preaching—not enough.

   (2) They had an overflowing fullness of the Holy Spirit—not like a cup half full, pathetically trying to run over.

   (3) They set an all time record of spiritual attractiveness and effectiveness.

   A certain pastor spoke of his church as being "small but spiritual." The terms are contradictory. A truly spiritual church can not remain small, but will draw people, like a holy magnet. Too often the world does not want what we have, because we do not have enough of it.

3. *Our preparation for revival must follow the Biblical pattern,* which has not changed since Pentecost.

   (1) The multitude marveled; perhaps they knew what the church had been, but not what it had become.

   (2) The Scriptures present *two VIEWS of the church,* with fifty days between:

I. FIFTY DAYS BEFORE PENTECOST, THE CHURCH WAS NOT READY FOR REVIVAL

1. *The fellowship was marred with petty bickering* (Luke 22:24). Same upper room, same persons, with same high mission—contending, "Who is greatest?"

2. *The leaders had slept in time of crisis* (Matt. 26:40). How could they sleep when Christ was in such agony of soul?

3. *The treasurer had sold his Lord for thirty pieces of silver*—Matt. 26:14-16; Luke 22:48. Three years of contact had left his heart unchanged, sordid, materialistic.

4. *The spokesman had denied Christ before His enemies*—John 18:25-27.

    The greater hindrance to spiritual power in the modern church is not outright denial of Christ, but inconsistent living. The life of a nominal Christian may be a stronger denial than his speech.

    A young child was asked, "Is your grandmother a Christian?" "Oh yes," was the prompt reply. To the next question, the reply was hesitant: "Is your mother a Christian?" "I don't know," said the child, "she says *she is." Inconsistencies which even a child can discern are not hidden from the Holy Spirit, who will not identify Himself with that which is unclean.*

5. *The church flock was scattered*—Matt. 26:56.

    What could be more dismal and depressing than a "dead" church!

    What greater proof of the divine intent, than its innumerable resurrections!

II. WHEN PENTECOST WAS "FULLY COME," THE CHURCH WAS READY

1. *Judas was dead;* in remorse he had "hanged himself" (Matt. 27:5).

    Cf.: One Jonah almost sank the ship (Jonah 1:12).

    Cf.: One Achan brought disaster to his people (Josh. 7).

2. *Peter had repented*—he "went out and wept bitterly" (Luke 22:62).

3. *The scattered flock was together "with one accord in one place"* (v. 1).

    Togetherness is the invariable pattern of spiritual revival; power cannot pass through broken wires; be reconciled—Matt. 5:21-24; 18:15.

4. *A great prayer meeting had been held*—Acts 1:12-14.

They prayed ten days and preached a few hours, and "three thousand souls" were added to that group of one hundred and twenty. In contrast, the typical church of today preaches ten days and prays a few hours, and requires a solid year for three thousand members to win one hundred and twenty souls to Christ. At Pentecost there were twenty-five additions per member, in one day; today there is one addition to twenty-five members in *one year!*

5. *A new power had been released*—"Ye shall receive power ... " (Acts 1:8).

The word *power* is translated from the Greek word *dunamis,* from which we have the word *dynamite.* Dynamite is not entrusted to undedicated, irresponsible persons.

CONCLUSION

Pentecostal power is conditioned on Pentecostal preparation.

1. The servants of Christ must come with clean hands (1 Tim. 5:22; Isa. 52:11).

2. The "fruit of the Spirit" must be real and visible (Gal. 5:22-23; Matt. 5:16).

3. The sacrifice must be upon the altar before the fire will fall from heaven.

Cf.: On Mount Carmel, the fire fell (I Kings 18:38); but not until Elijah had built an altar and laid his sacrifice upon it.

42. Motherhood at Its Best
(Mother's Day)

2 Kings 4:8-10, 18-27, 32-37

INTRODUCTION

1. *The little town of Shunem* is virtually unknown to us except for that modest home.

2. *The home* would never have been mentioned, but for the mother—"a great woman."

3. *The mother* is portrayed upon the background of one of the familiar sorrows of motherhood.

   (1) The child, playing in the field, exclaims, "My head, my head!" The father says, "Carry him to his mother." The child dies in the mother's lap. Gone is the joy of that home, the beauty of the hills, the inspiring majesty of Mount Tabor!

   (2) The mother does not despair; she knows what to do with her troubles. Like the Syrophenician woman who came to Jesus for help (Mark 7:25-30), this mother looks to the prophet of God.

4. *The portrayal of this mother* offers encouragement to worthy motherhood, by several REFLECTIONS of motherhood at its best:

I. HER FAITHFULNESS IN THE HOME

1. *The words of the father reflect full confidence in the mother—* "Carry him to his mother" (v. 19).

2. *The concern of the mother reflects true faithfulness.*

3. *The influence of a faithful mother is largely decisive in the life of the child.*

   (1) The child spends more hours under her care and tutelage than anywhere else.

(2) The home is the spiritual laboratory, where theory is tested in daily practice.

(3) The "self-made man" is probably more "home-made" than he realizes.

(4) The "hand that rocks the cradle, is the hand that rules the world."

The mother of John and Charles Wesley, a woman of extraordinary piety and prayer, gave to the world two sons who became spiritual giants. John became the founder of Methodism, and Charles became the writer of a rich treasury of hymns. Their combined labors have blessed multiplied millions for two centuries, and the blessings continue.

The mother of Abraham Lincoln died at the age of thirty-five, but she had already imparted such strength of character to her son as to insure his future. "All that I am or hope to be, I owe to my mother," was his grateful testimony in later years. Beside her humble grave at Lincoln City, Indiana, millions have bowed in reverence, upon reading the four words that declare her praise: "Mother of Abraham Lincoln."

II. HER STANDING WITH GOD

1. *The appraisal of the inspired writer* expresses more than a thousand ordinary eulogies—"a great woman" (v. 8).

2. *The restoration of the child* was plainly a gift of God.

   (1) It was not as a *man*, but as a *prophet of God*, that Elisha was able to help.

   (2) It was not for the *man*, but for the *man of God*, that Elisha was given lodging.

   (3) It was not the *hospitality* of the home, as such, that God was rewarding, but the *spiritual motivation* that prompted this hospitality.

3. *The response of God to this mother's grief* has been the response of God to the tears of many.

   Monica, the mother of the renowned Saint Augustine (354-430 A.D.), saw her son destroying his soul with sinful dissipation. She prayed with such tearful fervor that the Bishop of Carthage said to her, "Go thy way; it is impossible that the son of these tears should perish." There are no nobler lines in literature than the eulogies of that redeemed saint to his mother.

III. HER GIFT TO THE WORLD

1. *An example of spiritual perceptiveness—*"I perceive . . . " (v. 9). Others saw the same prophet, but did not "perceive."

    (1) The salvation of a home is often the spiritual perceptiveness of the mother, the one most likely to have it.

    (2) The depth of domestic tragedy is that of the household where none "perceive"—where bodies fatten and souls starve, overfed and undernourished.

    (3) The supreme contribution of mothers is not the biological fact of motherhood, or diligent care of bodies, but the mothering of souls, in a saving atmosphere.

2. *An example of spiritual service—*many hours of toil, but not in vain (Mark 9:41).

    (1) It related her to the God of the prophet, and opened the way to help from above.

    (2) It emphasized that long-established assurance, "Them that honour me, I will honour" (1 Sam. 2:30).

CONCLUSION

1. *A "great woman" of the Old Testament has spoken,* by her demonstration of motherhood at its best.

2. *A comparable example in the New Testament is that of the mother of Jesus—*"Mary, Queen of Mothers."

    (1) The best advice a mother ever gave: "Whatsoever he saith unto you, do it" (John 2:5).

    (2) The highest tribute with which to honor a mother: to live by this wise counsel.

43. A Day for Grateful Remembering (*Memorial Day*)

Mark 14:3-9

INTRODUCTION

1. *One of the richest gifts of God is the gift of memory.*

   (1) To relive past blessings.

   (2) To restore lost blessings (Rev. 2:5).

   (3) To warn and fortify against repetition of previous errors (Ps. 137:1).

2. *One of the noblest uses of memory: the recognition of our indebtedness to others.*

   This Gospel incident (Mark 14:3-9) carries two SUGGESTIONS for a worthy observance of Memorial Day:

I. LET THERE BE FLOWERS FOR THE DEPARTED

1. *The woman in this incident*—Mary of Bethany.

   For nearly two thousand years she has been memorialized, as Jesus implied that she should be—v. 9.

2. *The men who have given their lives in defense of our national heritage.*

   For nearly a century Americans have been observing Memorial Day in their honor.

3. *The founders of our country.*

   (1) The Pilgrims who came over on the Mayflower!

   Leaving their homeland for religious freedom, more precious to them than the comforts of home.

   Landing on the bleak shore of Cape Cod in winter, after sixty-four days of peril and misery, and falling on their knees in prayers of thanksgiving to God.

   Establishing a "Day of Thanksgiving" following their first full harvest.

(2) The writers of the Declaration of Independence—"With a firm reliance on the protection of Divine Providence, we mutually pledge to each other our lives, our fortunes, and our sacred honor."

(3) The "Father of our Country"—George Washington.

Kneeling in prayer in the snow of Valley Forge, seeking help from above.

Performing his first public act as president—going with the members of Congress, immediately after his inauguration, to the nearby St. Paul's Church on Broadway, where he led them in prayer.

Worshiping regularly on the Lord's Day in his own pew in St. Paul's Church.

(4) The framers of our Constitution. When the Constitutional Convention appeared to be hopelessly deadlocked, Benjamin Franklin called his fellow delegates to prayer; the deadlock was broken; the Constitution was adopted; the colonies were united.

4. *The persons who have preserved our spiritual heritage.*

Not only are we indebted to that long line of witnesses from apostolic times to our own day, but also to those who shared with us directly the knowledge of our Lord.

On the wall of my study is a wedding picture of my sister and brother-in-law, my father and mother, another sister, and some of our dearest friends of more than forty years ago. Two-thirds of the group have passed away, but the treasured memories remain. Again and again I have found myself pausing before that picture, in which I see my father and mother as I knew them best. Invariably my reaction, whether expressed in words or not, is a fervent "Thank You, Lord," and a new inspiration to "follow in their train." "The memory of the righteous is a blessing" (Prov. 10:7).

II. LET THERE BE FLOWERS FOR THE LIVING

1. *Jesus commends Mary for her lavish expression of gratitude and worship* (v. 9).

(1) Reflecting gratitude to Jesus for raising her brother Lazarus from the dead, less than thirty days before (John 11).

(2) Reflecting faith in the words of Jesus, soon to give His life—only three days later (v. 8).

(3) Reflecting a spiritual sensitivity exceeding that of the apostles.

2. *Jesus makes clear, the living deserve gratitude no less than the departed.*

   (1) Ingratitude is a common human failing.

   God repeatedly calls for remembrance, thanksgiving, praise (Ps. 103:2).

   God established aids to memory (Exod. 12:26-27; Josh. 4:6-7; 1 Cor. 11:24).

   (2) Silent appreciation is not enough—like a television program without sound.

   (3) Gratitude, warmly expressed, sweetens all relationships.

   (4) Time is running out—"Me ye have not always" (v. 7)—just three days left.

   In many a disturbed relationship the time for reconciliation is running out. Memorial Day may be a fortunate reminder—before it is too late.

   An ungrateful daughter who had deeply grieved her mother, and had never repaired the breach, was informed that the mother was critically ill. Now, for the first time, the daughter realized the urgency of setting things in order. She hurried back to the home which she had left, but it was too late. The mother lay in coma, and never regained consciousness. Words cannot express the grief and remorse of that daughter, sobbing at the bedside and crying, "If only I could talk to her for just one minute!" But it was not to be.

   With flowers for the living, Memorial Day can be the perfect occasion for healing impaired relationships.

CONCLUSION

Memorial Day can be a memorable day.

1. A day for remembering the departed who have blessed our lives, and the living.

2. A day for remembering our Savior, to whom we owe everything.

44. The Man or Woman of Tomorrow (*Children's Day*)

Luke 1:57-66

INTRODUCTION

1. *"What manner of child shall this be?"* This question, prompted by the extraordinary circumstances of the birth of John the Baptist, may appropriately be raised concerning every small child.

   (1) "Of such is the kingdom of God (Luke 18:16)—humble, trustful, receptive.

   (2) Of such are the future pillars of the church, the inspiring teachers and leaders of tomorrow.

   Before many a hallowed shrine, men and women bow in reverence and thank God for a life that began with no greater heritage than that of the child in our midst.

   (3) Of like tender beginnings are the future criminals, derelicts, racketeers.

   Outside the gray walls of a certain penitentiary is the prison graveyard, with rows of concrete slabs marking the inglorious end of lives that began with no lesser heritage than that of the child in our midst.

2. *What will determine the character and destiny of the child in our midst?* Will it be a comfort or a heartache; an inspiration or an evil influence; a blessing or a curse?

   The answer will depend on FACTORS in which we all are involved:

I. THAT WHICH THE PARENT SUPPLIES

"Bring them up in the nurture and admonition of the Lord" (Eph. 6:4).

1. *The character of the parent is usually transmitted to the child.*

2. *The power of the parent over the character and destiny of the child presents a fearful responsibility.*

3. *The most effective instruction may be by example.*

4. *The presence of the child in Sunday school is both a tribute and a prophecy.*

   A small child, lost and alone, was weeping on the street corner. A couple who were driving along that way paused and asked what her trouble was. "I want to go home," she said. But she did not know the way, or the name of the street, or the house number. She knew only her first name, and her parents were only "Mommie" and "Daddy." The couple followed one further cue: "Do you go to Sunday school?" Between sobs, the little one nodded. Then the further question, "If we took you to your Sunday school, could you find your way home?" Again, the little one nodded. And so she was taken to the nearest church, a few blocks away. As they drew up to the church and opened the door, the little one stepped out, and recognized her church. Without a further word, and with a shriek of delight, she ran down the street. The couple followed her to her home, a short distance away. No one needed to tell that couple what kind of a start that little one was being given by her dedicated, church-going parents.

II. THAT WHICH THE CHURCH SUPPLIES
"Go ye . . . make disciples . . . teaching them all things . . . "
(Matt. 28:19-20).
"Consider one another to provoke unto love
and to good works" (Heb. 10:24).

1. *The church cannot relieve the home of its responsibility* for the body, mind, and soul of the child (Deut. 6:6-7).

2. *The church is hardly less essential* to the salvation and nurture of the child. In the providence of God, the family altar and the family pew belong together.

3. *The church, like the parent, tends to mold the child in its own image.*

III. THAT WHICH THE CHILD SUPPLIES
"Continue thou in the things which thou hast learned . . . "
(2 Tim. 3:14-17).

1. *The deciding vote is cast by the child himself.*

   (1) Some of the shabbiest specimens of manhood and womanhood come from godly homes, with the benefit of spiritual churches and Sunday schools.

(2) Some of the noblest come from some of the shabbiest backgrounds.

Many instances come to mind, including that guest speaker whose radiant testimony was such a tremendous blessing to that Sunday morning audience. He did not tell his life story, but the chairman knew the facts, and revealed them afterwards. When the speaker was born, he was an unwanted child. He was wrapped in newspapers and dumped in an ash can along a back alley. Here, shortly afterwards, he was found by the "pick-up" crew, and was rescued. Such was the shabby beginning of a nobly dedicated life. The boy himself, in the course of time, cast the deciding vote, as he took the Lord Jesus into his heart.

2. *The deciding factor may be an alert, spiritually concerned teacher.*

CONCLUSION

1. *The parent or teacher does not labor alone,* however obscure the setting. " . . . lo, I am with you always . . . " (Matt. 28:20).

2. *The fruitage may be delayed,* but "my word . . . shall not return unto me void" (Isa. 55:11).

3. *The rewards are everlasting.* (Dan. 12:3).

4. *The child in our midst is included in that blessed invitation,* "Come unto me . . . " (Luke 18:16).

45. Godliness Begins at Home
(Father's Day)

Joshua 24:13-18

INTRODUCTION

1. *Joshua concludes with this testimony, his powerful and fruitful appeal to Israel* (v. 15).

2. *Joshua had the benefit of several favoring factors.*

    (1) He knew the history of his people—enslaved in Egypt, wandering in the wilderness, crossing the Jordan, occupying the Promised Land.

    (2) He spoke with the authority of experience—walked with Moses 40 years, inherited his responsibilities, bore them for 25 years, was now 110 years old.

    (3) He chose the perfect setting for his farewell appeal—Shechem was alive with hallowed memories—Abraham's altar (Gen. 12:6-7); Jacob's well (John 4:6); and here, between Mount Ebal and Mount Gerizim, that tremendous dedication service had taken place 25 years before (Josh. 8:33; Deut. 27:9-26).

    (4) He reinforced his appeal with the power of a good example—"as for me. . . ."

3. *Joshua's testimony gives INSIGHTS into the spiritual life of a man approved and mightily used of God:*

I. HE ACKNOWLEDGES HIS RESPONSIBILITY FOR THE SPIRITUAL LIFE OF HIS FAMILY
" . . . as for me and my house. . . ."

1. *The family is designed of God to be the basic educational unit.*

    (1) Moses had spelled out God's pattern 25 years before (Deut. 6:6-9; 11:18-21).

    (2) Paul, the apostle, gives the same emphasis—"bring them up" (Eph. 6:4).

2. *The family will usually follow the parent, especially the father.*

   (1) At home, no substitute for parental communication, time, attention.
   Hunger for attention accounts for much juvenile vandalism and rebellion.

   (2) At church, rarely is the mother less faithful than the father. A pastor, emphasizing his Men's Bible Class, remarked: "If we have the child in Sunday school, that may be all; if we have the mother, we have the mother and the child, and that may be all; if we have the father, we have the father, the mother, the child, and the family car enlisted on the Lord's side."

II. HE INDICATES A PLAN FOR THE SPIRITUAL LIFE OF HIS FAMILY—
" . . . we will serve the Lord."

1. *A godly example, the most eloquent instruction of all.*

   In my earliest childhood I was imbued with reverence for the Bible as the Word of God, and the church as the house of God; and Sabbath observance was taken for granted. Yet I cannot recall a single instance of being taught these things by word of mouth. They were constantly exemplified by my father and mother. The same was true of tithing. When I began lifelong tithing, I had never been told that I should tithe, and I had never heard a sermon on the subject. But I had known from early childhood that my father was a regular tither, and that the practice of tithing was taught in the Bible; and that was enough! Truly, the most effective schooling on earth is that which is imparted, by example, in the home!

2. *A family altar suggested.*

   (1) The indispensable elements in spiritual well-being: private devotions, group devotions, and family devotions.

   (2) The time to set up family devotions: the first day of marriage.

3. *A united family*—"me and my house."

   (1) No tie so binds as for the marriage partners to be sincerely devoted to the Lord.

   (2) No cleavage is so deep, so wide, and so decisive as for one of the partners to be walking up the high road that leads to the

heavenly home, while the other is walking down the low road that leads to a Christless, Saviorless, hopeless eternity.

III. HE EXPRESSES A GODLY DETERMINATION TO PERSEVERE, WITH HIS FAMILY

1. *Joshua was prepared to stand alone if necessary.*

   (1) It would not be the first time he had stood apart from the multitude.
   At Kadesh-Barnea, 65 years before—Caleb and Joshua (Num. 14:6-10
   With God on his side, he would always be in the majority.

2. *Joshua was determined at least to establish a spiritual oasis with his family.*
   In such oases, spiritual giants are grown.

CONCLUSION

1. *Godliness begins at home.*

2. *Godliness brings blessedness*—"Them that honour me, I will honour" (1 Sam. 2:30).

An aged minister was relating one of the most memorable experiences of his long, eventful ministry. In one of the towns where he served as pastor, there was a notoriously hardened saloon keeper. He never attended church, and was utterly unapproachable on spiritual matters. But one day the pastor was overwhelmed with astonishment as the saloon keeper came to him and abruptly announced, "I want to become a Christian, and I want you to show me the way!" What had happened? His wife had been a Christian for some time, and the husband, observing her life at close range, had concluded, "She has something that I don't have, and I want what she has!" Another demonstration that the most powerful sermons are not preached, but lived!

144

46. Bread for the Soul
(*Labor Day*)

Isaiah 55

INTRODUCTION

1. *God is not indifferent to the sorrows, sufferings, and struggles of His people.*

    (1) Where there was bereavement, "Jesus wept" (John 11:35).

    (2) Where there was suffering, He healed (Matt. 9:35).

    (3) Where there was weariness from excessive toil, He said, "Come unto me" (Matt. 11:28).

2. *God is not lacking in resources to meet human need.*

    (1) "The world is mine, and the fulness thereof" (Ps. 50:12).

    (2) "The silver is mine, and the gold is mine ... " (Hag. 2:8).

    (3) " ... the cattle upon a thousand hills" (Ps. 50:10).

3. *God is not thinking primarily of bread for the body, but bread for the soul.*

4. *God, in calling His people to higher ground, spells out the ALTERNATIVES:*

I. THE HUNGER THAT COMES THROUGH DISOBEDIENCE

1. *In disobedience, labor is fruitless*—"Wherefore ... for that ... " (v. 2)?

    (1) Haggai 1:6—"sow much, harvest little; eat and drink ... not filled."

    (2) Amos 2:9—God "destroyed his fruit from above, and his roots from beneath."

    (3) Psalm 127:1—"Except the Lord build the house, they labour in vain. . . ."

2. *In disobedience, money is unavailing*—"satisfieth not" (v. 2).

(1) Money is admittedly a power not to be despised.

It enables the faithful steward to evangelize to the ends of the earth.

It nourishes Christian enterprises which would cease to function without it.

(2) Money can buy physical comforts, but not bread for the soul.

The "rich fool" amassed great wealth, but lost his soul (Luke 12:20).

Many a *"poor fool"* has come to the same sad ending—without even the momentary satisfactions of amassed wealth.

History abounds in instances of fabulous wealth coupled with poverty of soul. Typical is the case of that prince in India who died possessed of a massive fortune, and was buried in his gorgeous robe, with his jewels, in a magnificant marble tomb. Nearby, his horse was buried, and his sword, a jug of water, and dishes of food. The musicians played, and dancing girls whirled for weeks. But what about his soul? "What shall it profit a man . . . " (Mark 8:36)?

II. THE SATISFACTION THAT COMES THROUGH OBEDIENCE

1. *It is not necessary to remain unfed.*

    (1) "Come unto *me* . . . " (v. 3); "I am thy *God*" (Isa. 41:10).

    (2) "Hearken . . . unto *me* " (v. 2). Perhaps, overfed and undernourished, you have tried every unsatisfying substitute, and are still uneasily moving around "like an accident, going somewhere to happen."

2. *It is not necessary to remain unforgiven* (v. 6-7; Isa. 1:18).

    (1) The heaviest load of all is that of unconfessed, unremoved, unforgiven sin.

    (2) The crushing burden of Christian, in "Pilgrim's Progress," rolled from his shoulders when he came to the foot of the cross—"Thy sins be forgiven thee!"

3. *It is not necessary to remain uncomforted.*

    (1) "Go out with joy" (v. 12).

Cf.: Sad faces on mission field, skid row, and highest levels of society, reflecting godlessness and hopelessness.

(2) "Arise, shine . . . the glory of the Lord is risen upon thee" (Isa. 60:1).

CONCLUSION

1. *All around us are evidences of the love of God, which only the obedient can see.*

   "Except a man be born again, he can not see . . . " (John 3:3); and only he that "willeth to do His will" shall know . . . (John 7:17, ASV). Isaiah was in the temple when he saw the Lord (Isa. 6). He saw himself, confessed his uncleanness, received cleansing, heard the call of God—and a new life was begun. But not even in the Lord's temple is there illumination for the unwilling.

   The soldiers of Napoleon stabled their horses in the beautiful cathedral of Strassburg. They had no eyes for the stained glass windows, no ears for the ringing of the bell, no feeling for the altar with its invitation to prayer. They did not sense the loving presence of the living God.

2. *All of life can be a triumphal march* (v. 12).

   (1) "The path of the just is as the shining light, that shineth more and more unto the perfect day" (Prov. 4:18).

   (2) The glory in the distance recalls the glory of creation, "when the morning stars sang together, and all the sons of God shouted for joy" (Job 38:7).

47. A Song of Thanksgiving
(Thanksgiving Day)

Psalm 118:1, 14-24, 29

INTRODUCTION

"O give thanks unto the Lord, for He is good; for His mercy endureth forever."

1. *This outburst of praise and thanksgiving is associated with the darkest night in the earthly life of the Lord Jesus Christ.*

    (1) In the solemnity of the upper room, He had dramatized His impending death; He had foretold the unfaithfulness of Peter, the treachery of Judas; and Judas had gone out.

    (2) Ahead, lay the grim shadows of Gethsemane; then, that fateful Friday; and that sad, silent Saturday . . .

    (3) In that total blackout, the Lord Jesus, with His disciples matching His spirit, broke the silence with such singing as would never suggest its tragic setting (Matt. 26:30). The "hymn" is believed to have been Psalm 118, a ringing summons to praise and thanksgiving, in use for four hundred years, like our Doxology, for great days of national rejoicing. "This is the day . . . " (v. 24).

2. *This outburst of praise and thanksgiving arises from two powerful inspirations.* With the lift of these INSPIRATIONS, singing is possible even in days of gloom, grief, and disaster:

I. THE INSPIRATION OF A FAR LOOK
" . . . his mercy endureth forever" (v. 1, 29).

1. *The psalmist did not build the psalm on some passing phase of human experience.*

2. *Jesus did not sing the psalm in the inspiration of present circumstances* (Heb. 12:2; Phil. 2:9-11).

3. *Followers of Christ must likewise find their inspiration in the far look* (Rom. 8:18, 28; I Cor. 2:9).

(1) Not much in the immediate present to sing about. But thank God (Hab. 2:14).

(2) Not much in the immediate past to sing about. But "in everything give thanks" (I Thess. 5:18).

It is related of the renowned Bible commentator Matthew Henry that he was once the victim of an armed robbery. But he came out of the experience with praise and thanksgiving, for several reasons: First, that the robbers had taken his money, and not his life; second, that although they took all that he had, the amount was not large; third, that he was the victim *of the robbery, and not the* perpetrator.

(3) Not much in the immediate future to sing about. But "be anxious in nothing" (Phil. 4:6-7).

Above the clouds, the sun is shining. Beyond the shadows, a golden daybreak awaits the believer. In the Scriptures are many "Fear nots," all addressed to believers. Bible students have counted 365 such passages. This means that there is a fresh "Fear not" for every day of the year. A speaker challenged her audience to go to their Bibles and find the 365 "Fear nots," beginning with Gen. 15:1 and ending with Rev. 1:17-18. A woman reported later, "I have finished my home work and I have found every "Fear not." "I am a changed woman . . . have never known relief from fear until now." A beautiful fulfillment of the divine purpose!

II. THE INSPIRATION OF A RETENTIVE MEMORY
"O give thanks unto the Lord, for He is good . . . " (v. 1, 29).

1. *In the opening strain, the psalmist recalls the everlasting goodness of God;* in the closing refrain, he makes the same acknowledgement.

2. *Between the two, shines the middle verse of the Bible—*"It is better to trust in the Lord than to put confidence in man" (v. 8).

(1) It carries the supreme lesson of human history.

(2) It calls to mind the supreme fact of this universe: "The Lord God omnipotent reigneth" (Rev. 19:6); and He will have the last word.

"The stone which the builders rejected is become the head . . . " (v. 22).

"They are dead that sought the young child's life" (Matt. 2:20).

They that reject Christ are paying unwilling tribute to Him, in the dating of every letter, every contract, and every check—"A.D. 19___."

CONCLUSION

The psalm that Jesus sang sets the tone for perennial thanksgiving—"O give thanks" (v. 1).

1. *"Every good gift is from above* . . . from the Father . . . " (James 1:17).

2. *Every day is "Thanksgiving Day"* when the heart is rightly attuned.

48. The Doxology of the Angels (*Christmas*)

Luke 2:8-20.

INTRODUCTION

A little girl was taken to an elegant department store by a "rich uncle" who was going to buy her a lavish Christmas gift. From a fabulous display of gifts, she was to choose anything that she wanted, and it would be bought for her, regardless of size or price. Delighted, and overwhelmed by the profusion of gifts, she began shopping around. A salesman, with the prospect of an extraordinary sale, did his utmost to be helpful; and after a while the manager of the department also gave assistance. After hovering endlessly over a wide selection, including the most elaborate and expensive gifts, the little girl reached a conclusion. "Do you mean," she asked, "that I can really have anything I want—just anything?" Being reassured, she said, "Then, this is what I want." Retracing her steps, she picked up and tenderly pressed to her bosom a tiny plush squirrel, priced at twenty-five cents!

1. *Too many people get too little out of Christmas.*

    (1) For some, nothing more than profitable merchandizing—not angels singing, but singing commercials.

    (2) For some, only a holiday, with a carnival spirit and a dissipating round of social functions.

    (3) For some, only a hectic scramble for Christmas gifts and Christmas trees.

2. *Too many people never experience real Christmas joy.*

    (1) The angel preacher said, "I bring you good tidings of great joy."

    There *was* joy for the shepherds, the virgin mother, and the wise men.

    But not all shepherds left their flocks; not all wise men saw the star; the villagers slept; and the inn keeper missed a great opportunity.

    (2) The angel preacher emphasized, this joy was "to all people."

Cf.: Ocean tide flowing into harbor, lifting every craft, every size.

(3) The angel chorus added something essential: "glory . . . peace . . . good will."
This "Doxology" gives divine formula for perfect Christmas, in two PARTS:

I. LET EVERY OBSERVANCE BE TO THE GLORY OF GOD

1. *This lifts our Christmas far above the ordinary holidy atmosphere,* with revelry and excesses which profane this holy season.

2. *This places Christ at the center*—"He that honoureth not the Son honoureth not the Father" (John 5:23).

3. *This places Christ at the head of the Christmas list.*
   "The one thing that we enjoy most, at Christmas time," said the wife of a prominent businessman, "is the distribution of gifts to needy Christian causes." This was over and above their monthly program of systematic giving. By Christmastime they knew fairly well the outcome of the year's operations; they knew their abilities, and were ready to enjoy this high point of their celebration.

II. LET EVERY OBSERVANCE BE TO THE FURTHERANCE OF "PEACE AND GOOD WILL"

1. *A time to pray, "Let there be peace on earth, and let it begin with me."*

2. *A time for strengthening old ties and building bridges to new friends.*
   The sending of Christmas cards, begun in 1842, has marvelous possibilities.
   "May friendships grow dearer, life's meaning be clearer, and heaven come nearer—at Christmas!"

3. *A time for repairing injured relationships.*

   (1) The only balm for a soul that has sinned is forgiveness.
   Time cannot heal; the only therapy that works is the therapy which Jesus prescribed (Matt. 5:23-24).

   (2) The only balm for a soul that has been sinned against is forgiveness; hence, the therapy of Jesus (Matt. 18:15-17).

Better, one note asking or extending forgiveness than a thousand perfunctory greeting cards.

Better, one real reconciliation than the distribution of truck-loads of expensive gifts.

CONCLUSION

1. *The way to fullness of Christmas joy is not by some secret formula,* but by responding to the "Doxology of the Angels."

    (1) Receiving, with Christ left out, leaves the heart empty.

    (2) Giving, however lavish, with Christ left out, leaves the heart hungry.

2. *The fullness of Christmas joy is available to every empty life, every hungry heart.*

    An elderly woman, who was approaching her "three-score-and-ten," was still spending several evenings a week in volunteer service at a rescue mission for "down-and-outers" in New York City. Looking back over a wealth of happy Christmas memories, she pointed to one Christmas as the greatest in her long and eventful life. It was that Christmas when, as a young woman, she had been persuaded to attend an evening service at the mission, which afterwards became one of the greatest concerns of her life. Here, on that first visit, she had made the saving contact with the Christ of Christmas, the hope of empty lives and broken hearts.

49. A Slave Who Met Every Test

Genesis 37:1-4, 12-14, 23-24, 28, 36.

INTRODUCTION

Jacob "loved Joseph more than all his children, because he was the son of his old age" (Gen. 37:3).

1. *When Joseph's brothers saw this they "envied" him* (v. 11) *and "hated" him* (v. 4).

2. *When Joseph was sent to his brothers in the field they "cast him into a pit."*

3. *When the Midianites came along he was sold to them for twenty pieces of silver.*

4. *When the Midianites got to Egypt they sold Joseph to Potiphar*, an officer of Pharaoh, a "captain of the guard" (v. 36).

Thus began the career of this seventeen-year-old slave, who met the *TESTS* of life in a way that has blessed many generations.

I. HE WAS TESTED IN THE HOUSE OF POTIPHAR

1. *His relationship to God made him a blessing to the house of Potiphar* (vv. 3, 5).

   (1) This recalls the blessing that his father, Jacob, was to the house of Laban (Gen. 30:27).

   (2) This blessing still follows consistent godly living, as reflected in a recent tribute: "I am a better Christian because of my association with this dear friend."

2. *His relationship to God saved Joseph when the wife of Potiphar tried to tempt him.*

   (1) The only way to security is the Biblical way — "wait upon the Lord" (Isa. 40:31).

   (2) The experience of many believers is reflected in that familiar hymn: "I need Thee every hour, Stay Thou near by; temptations lose their power when Thou art nigh."

II. HE WAS TESTED IN THE EGYPTIAN PRISON

1. *Here, as when he was sold into slavery, he might have become embittered.*

   But "the Lord was with him, and that which he did, the Lord made it to prosper" (Gen. 39:23).

2. *Here was perhaps the greatest piece of good fortune that ever happened to him.*

   "All things work together for good to them that love God" (Rom. 8:28).

3. *Here he interpreted the dreams of Pharaoh's butler and his baker.*

   This brought him to the attention of Pharaoh, and ultimately to a position of power (Gen. 41:41).

III. HE WAS TESTED IN THE HOUSE OF PHARAOH

1. *This was probably the greatest test of all*, with Pharaoh acknowledging the hand of God, and elevating Joseph to the second highest position in the empire.

2. *This might have been Joseph's undoing.*

   (1) To come to such power, from abject slavery, might have produced pride.

   (2) To have his brothers at his mercy, after their cruel mistreatment of him, might have led to revenge.

3. *This test led to Joseph's crowning achievement:*

   (1) Reconciliation with his brethren.

   "Ye thought evil against me; but the Lord meant it unto good . . . to save much people alive" (Gen. 50:20).

   (2) Resettlement of his family in Egypt, for the duration of the famine in their homeland.

CONCLUSION

1. *Joseph spent many years in a world totally alien to his Lord, yet he was never alone.* "The Lord was with him" (Gen. 39:3). Before each chapter closes there is evidence that others came to this realiza-

tion. How easily Joseph could have fallen into the pattern of those around him. His family was faraway, and there were no believers with whom to have fellowship.

2. *Joseph, walking with his Lord, was a ceaseless blessing to the lives that he touched and to posterity.*

50. A Shepherd Who Became a King

1 Samuel 16:7-13

INTRODUCTION

1. *It was a notable day on that quiet sheep ranch in the hills of Judea, with three surprises:*

    (1) The family of Jesse was honored with a visit by a distinguished guest.

    (2) He came to identify and anoint the future king of Israel.

    (3) He chose the youngest of eight sons, who was not even present.

2. *It was a choice not hard to understand when we know something about that "stripling"* (1 Sam. 17:56).

    (1) God chose David for the position of king.

    (2) God saw in David the *QUALITIES* which made for greatness.

I. HE WAS A WORKER
"He keepeth the sheep" (v. 11).

1. *God cannot use a shirker.*

    Moses was busy as a shepherd when God called him (Exod. 3:1).

    Gideon was threshing wheat (Judg. 6:11).

    Elisha was plowing (1 Kings 19:19).

    Four of the apostles were fishing and mending nets (Matt. 4:18-22).

2. *"Whatsoever thy hand findeth to do, do it with thy might"* (Eccles. 9:10).

3. *"Whatsoever ye do, do it heartily, as to the Lord. . . ."* (Col. 3:23).

II. HE WAS DEPENDABLE

1. *When Samuel came, the father had no doubts as to David's whereabouts.*
2. *When prowling beasts came, he was on the job* (1 Sam. 17:34-35).

III. HE HAD GOOD HABITS

1. *David, while "keeping the sheep," developed some important skills:*

   (1) He became skillful with the harp, skillful enough to play before the king.

   (2) He became skillful with the slingshot — to protect his sheep, and to meet the giant Goliath.

   (3) He became skillful in poetry, as reflected in the psalms.

2. *Psychologists have pointed out that habit can be a substantial aid to godliness.*

   Becoming a Christian involves the adoption of a godly lifestyle, and bringing every activity into the pattern. Therefore, the strong initiative suggested by the command of Jesus to "confess him before men," and to receive baptism. "Thus it becometh us to fulfill all righteousness" (Matt. 3:15). Then, let there be no exception till the habit is securely rooted, with continuous exercise thereafter to keep the good habits vital. No lifestyle is secure until it has become habitual.

IV. HE HAD A GOOD REPUTATION

1. *When the King needed a harpist,* he called for David because his reputation had reached from the hills of Judea to the halls of the palace (1 Sam. 16:18).

2. *Sooner or later a person's reputation catches up with his character.*

   (1) Every national election brings this to remembrance.

   (2) Many critical issues are settled on the basis of reputation.

   Years ago a particularly complicated lawsuit was being fought out before a judge and jury. The outcome was utterly unpredictable. Ultimately it became a matter of choosing which of two opposing witnesses to believe. The outcome of the trial was settled entirely on this basis, and later developments vindicated the decision of the jury.

V. HE HAD A CLEAN HEART

1. *God sees all, hears all, remembers all, makes no mistakes.*

   "David behaved himself wisely . . . and the Lord was with him" (1 Sam. 18:14).

2. God *"sought him a man after his own heart"* (1 Sam. 13:14).

   David was that man — "a man after [His] own heart" (Acts 13:22).

CONCLUSION

1. *The time to prepare for promotion is long before the opening occurs.*

2. *The time to build a reputation is long before the need arises.*

51. A Little Maid in Syria

2 Kings 5:1-10, 14-15

INTRODUCTION

1. *How little?* *The context suggests less than full grown.*

2. *How profoundly she affected the household is not left in doubt.*

   Involved was "the captain of the host of Syria," and then "the king of Syria."

3. *How she attained to such tremendous influence is not spelled out.*

   An unlikelier counselor to an empire's commander-in-chief could hardly be imagined. She was a slave from a foreign, despised people.

4. *How her testimony bore fruit is suggested in four BRIGHT SPOTS that stand out as the story unfolds:*

I. SHE KNEW THE LORD EARLY IN LIFE

1. *An early relationship with the Lord will save from innumerable errors,* losses, and regrets along the way.

   (1) Life is lived on a one-way street, and is irreversible.

   (2) The record we write remains written, as if we were walking on wet concrete.

2. *An early knowledge of Scripture is profitable* (2 Tim. 3:15-17).

   Scriptures memorized in childhood often come alive after many years, to the salvation of the soul.

II. SHE WAS READY TO WITNESS WHEN THE MOMENT CAME (v. 3)

1. *Such is the divine intent* (Acts 1:8).

   Every believer ought to be alert, concerned, vocal; thus revival would sweep the land.

2. *Such is not the prevailing pattern* — too much silence.

A man who was a department superintendent in the Sunday school was enthusiastically telling his pastor about a fellow-workman whom he found to be likewise a department superintendant as busy as he himself. "Wonderful," said the pastor, "how long have you been working together?" "About three months," was the reply. Then the pastor broke in with this blunt question: "What's wrong with both of you? Is it possible that you two could work side by side for three months and not care enough to inquire whether the other is a child of God on the way to heaven, or a lost sinner on the way to hell?"

III. SHE SO LIVED AS TO GAIN THE CONFIDENCE OF HER SUPERIORS

1. *She did not permit herself to become embittered.*

2. *She did not bear malice toward her master.*

3. *She did not lose her faith in God.*

4. *She did not win her case with a single testimony.*

The "little maid in Syria" had much in common with Naomi, who, with her husband and two sons, took refuge in the idolatrous land of Moab during a time of famine in their homeland. Here, after several years, the husband and sons of Naomi died, and she prepared to return to her homeland. Ruth, her daughter-in-law, refused to be separated from her. "Intreat me not to leave thee . . . thy people shall be my people, and *thy God my God*" (Ruth 1:16). Such is the eloquence of consistent godly living in a pagan environment.

IV. SHE SAW HER FAITH REWARDED

1. *The physical healing of Naaman was itself a tremendous reward.*

His flesh was "clean like the flesh of a little child."

2. *The spiritual blessing was far greater and more lasting* — "now I know" (v. 15).

"With joy shall ye draw water out of the wells of salvation" (Isa. 12:3).

CONCLUSION

The "little maid in Syria" set an inspiring example for all believers.

(1) We are a colony of heaven (Phil. 3:20).

(2) We are called and appointed to "let our light shine" (Matt. 5:16).

52. A Boy Who Shared His Lunch

John 6:1-13

INTRODUCTION

1. *One unexpected guest at mealtime would throw many a housewife into a panic.*

   Here, 5,000 unexpected guests produced no panic, but a miracle. The crisis was met, the hungry fed, and an abundance left over.

2. *Many important people must have been here, but the most important, except Jesus, was this lad with the loaves and fishes.*

   (1) There is no indication of his name, age, or background; but the incident is rich in implications.

   (2) There are four *WAYS* in which he set a good example for all boys, girls, men, and women:

I. HE RAN WITH THE RIGHT CROWD

1. *It is always safe to follow the crowd that is following Jesus.*

   (1) Christ is honored. "Where I am, there shall also my servant be" (John 12:26).

   "Them that honor me, I will honor. . . ." (1 Sam. 2:30).

   (2) Believers are strengthened against the hazards along the King's highway.

   "Those are my best friends in whose presence I can be my best self."

   (3) Strangers are most likely to come to the knowledge of Christ when in the company of believers.

2. *There are always two crowds.*

   (1) A small dedicated minority of believers — how naturally they gravitate together (Mal. 3:16-17).

163

(2) A large unwashed majority who seek pleasure, popularity, "lusts of the flesh."

(3) "Blessed is the man who walketh not . . . nor standeth . . . nor sitteth. . . ." (Ps. 1).

(4) Peter never fell so low as when he "sat down among" the enemies of Christ (Luke 22:55-62).

A boy in a suburb of Chicago got into serious trouble, and was convicted and sentenced. The mother made a highly emotional appeal to the judge. "He was such a good boy; he just got into bad company." She was forgetting that when a good boy gets into bad company, he ceases to be a good boy. The same is true of the good girl or the good man or good woman.

(4) "Blessed is the man who" never did. . . .

The law of the harvest has never been repealed—what we sow, we reap.

The consequence of past misdeeds can never be fully erased. Samson was probably the strongest man in the world, but he went wrong. He was taken by the Philistines who put out his eyes. His strength was largely restored, but his eyes never came back (Judg. 16:21, 30).

II. HE LOOKED AHEAD

1. *"Boys will be boys" and boys will be men; but what kind of men?*

(1) The boy casts the deciding vote.

(2) The boy fixes the direction. "Be kind to the man you're going to be."

(3) The boy who goes straight is like the tree that grows tall and straight.

2. *Boys who look ahead don't say, "I'll try anything once."*

(1) Once is one time too much if it grieves or offends the Lord (1 Cor. 3:16).

(2) Once done, it may lead to a sinful habit—drunkenness, drug addiction, etc.

III. HE DARED TO BE DIFFERENT

1. *He was probably the only person in that multitude who carried a lunch.*

   The willingness to be different is often a test of character (Rom. 12:2).

2. *He was not the only youth in Scripture who dared to stand alone.*

   (1) Daniel did not say, "When in Babylon, do as the Babylonians do"; but "Daniel purposed in his heart that he would not defile himself" (Dan. 1:8).

   (2) Joseph, sold into slavery in Egypt, did not forget his Lord (Gen. 39:5).

   (3) The "little maid in Syria" was a real blessing to that household (2 Kings 5).

IV. HE TRUSTED THE LORD JESUS

1. *He put all that he had in the hands of Jesus.*

   There is no provision in Scripture for halfway, part-time, short-term Christians, or for retirement with fringe benefits.

2. *He did not go away hungry.*

   Lunch for one boy became a meal for five thousand. Little is much if God is in it.

CONCLUSION

1. *What a precious experience and what a treasured memory* for the boy who shared his lunch!

2. *How beautifully this experience repeats itself with those who trust Jesus!*

   Typical is the experience of that famous millionaire who declared, toward the end of his life, "I have often been in transactions involving millions of dollars; but by far the greatest transaction of my life occurred when, as a small boy, I committed myself to Jesus Christ as my Lord and Savior."